# FAITH, HOPE, LOVE, KNITTING

# FAITH, HOPE, LOVE,

## Knitting

Celebrating the Gift of Knitting

with 24 Beautiful Patterns

LORNA MISER Founder of LORNA'S LACES

WATSON-GUPTILL PUBLICATIONS/NEW YORK

Executive Editor: Joy Aquilino

Editor: Martha Moran

Art Director: Jess Morphew

Production Manager: Alyn Evans

Photographer: Simon Lee

Book and cover designer and photo shoot art director: Chin-Yee Lai

Published in the United States by Watson-Guptill Publications,

an imprint of the Crown Publishing Group, a division of Random House, Inc., New York.

www.crownpublishing.com

www.watsonguptill.com


**Library of Congress Cataloging-in-Publication Data is available from the Library of Congress**

Miser, Lorna.

   Faith, hope, love, knitting : celebrating the gift of knitting with 24

beautiful patterns / Lorna Miser.

      p. cm.

   Includes index.

   ISBN 978-0-8230-9952-8 (pbk.)

1.  Knitting--Patterns.  I. Title.

   TT825.M59 2009

   746.43'2041--dc22

                              2008035068

ISBN 10: 0-8230-9952-0

ISBN 13: 978-0-8230-9952-8


Printed in China



1 2 3 4 5 6 7 8 9 / 17 16 15 14 13 12 11 10 09


First Edition

# Dedication

**M**y life changed a lot during the making of this book. Over that time I became a more confident Lorna. I'm happy and true to myself and I like my life and who I am. I would like to honor all women who take charge of their own lives and are courageous enough to choose a life in which they can be honest and true to themselves, to show their full personality with pride and fulfillment. I especially thank Joy for her encouragement and for reminding me that although my life had changed courses, my faith had not. I remain deeply in love with my God and am assured of His love for me. Other things in life change, but this does not.

Because I was going through some of the most difficult times of my life during the writing of this book, I survived with the encouragement of friends like Monica, Frederikka, Sheila, and Joy. I completed all of the knitting because of the talents of Grace, Kimberly, Sheila, Sandi, André, and Lori. I love and need all of you as friends and sisters. God bless all of you and I thank Him for each of you.

Love,
Lorna

Me at age 6 with my grandma Helen Oberheu, who unknowingly kindled the spark that would inspire me to develop one of my creative gifts.

# CONTENTS

# Preface

As I approach a group of friends at my local coffee shop, they notice I'm wearing a handknit sweater that I recently finished. One of them comments that she doesn't have the patience to learn to knit. Another is sure that she'll never move beyond knitting a scarf. Another friend prefers crochet. What they're all really trying to say is that they admire the sweater and my ability to make it. Each friend has different skills and interests—cooking, reading, gardening, raising animals—so it amuses me that they see my gift, my God-given ability and passion, as somehow different from their own.

My gift is knitting. It's a wonderful, exciting, creative gift from God, so I use it a lot. In fact, I take my knitting everywhere, not to show off my talent or to draw attention to myself, but because it's so much a part of who I am. I knit in places where it's considered "normal" and "acceptable," such as doctors' waiting rooms (to make good use of the time I spend waiting) and knitting guild meetings (where lots of other people are knitting). But I also knit virtually everywhere else I go. I knit at church. I knit while waiting in line at Wal-Mart. I knit at the coffee shop. I knit at the movie theater. I knit in restaurants. I knit at the amusement park while waiting in long lines for the highest roller coasters. I knit when road construction is holding up traffic. I've knit on every airplane I've ever been on, and on every trip I've ever taken. I've even knit during labor for each of my three kids and while waiting for surgery.

If you're a knitter, you've either knit in some of the same places and under the same circumstances, or you think I need to join a support group for my knitting addiction. Well, it's true—I love to knit. But knitting practically everywhere is for me more than just a way to pass time productively, or to make headway on a project. There's something even better that comes from my knitting than anything I can make with yarn: It's the constant flow of new friendships that grow because of those sticks that I'm holding in my hands. My knitting has opened countless conversations, sparked numerous interesting encounters with strangers, given me many opportunities to share meaningful time with people, and afforded me more friends than I can count (or whose names I can recall). But the time I spend with each person I meet is precious, and the memories I have of our connection priceless, no matter how brief. Each person has been in the right place at the right time, for a reason—and I've been there, knitting, with a story to tell or an ear to lend, also for a reason. This book tells many of those stories. Each story includes a knitting project I've designed that commemorates that cherished memory.

The gifts of knitting have brought many blessings to my life. So join me as we visit with friends and family, laugh, and sometimes cry, all while knitting!

# FAITH, HOPE,

# LOVE,

# KNITTING

# GRANDMA HELEN's
# LACE

I guess you could say that knitting runs in my family. My mother is a knitter, and my Grandma Helen—my mother's mother—was a knitter and a seamstress. She was also practical and frugal. Unlike me, whose yarn stash far exceeds what I could ever knit (it fills several walls of floor-to-ceiling shelves), she never accumulated a supply of yarn or fabric. She bought materials as she needed them for each project, worked on one project at a time, and used up every scrap before buying more supplies or starting another project.

One of the few things she did for pure pleasure was knit lace doilies. She would have a doily on her needles—or "knitting pins," as she called them—at all times. All those sharp metal double-points poking every which way sure looked intimidating! But every day or two she would finish another doily, starch it with her own secret recipe (she cooked up the starch herself), pin it out to the right shape, and mount it on a piece of cardboard covered with tissue paper. Then my shy, quiet Grandma would take her doilies to the bank or the beauty parlor, and show her knitting to the teller or the hairdresser or to one of the other customers. Her excitement about her work was obvious, and her passion for her lace creations helped her overcome her shyness. She would make a sale every time, and even get orders for more. I was so proud of her.

Grandma Helen was convinced that she wasn't a teacher, so she didn't believe that she could teach me how to knit lace. But teaching can be done in many ways. She let me stand behind her chair while she cast on the stitches, masterfully manipulating all those needles that kept slipping, and showed me how to use a crochet hook to bind off the lacy edging around the doily's perimeter. She unwittingly taught me to knit in the "German" or Continental style, holding the yarn in my left hand and hooking it with the tip of the right needle.

I love lace, especially knitted lace, and I'm so glad that Grandma Helen didn't tell me that it was too hard when I was a beginner knitter. She passed on her knowledge and the tradition to me. Years later, when I added a lace-weight yarn to Lorna's Laces, I named it "Helen's Lace" in honor of my favorite lace knitter.

# Grandma's Lace Shawl

Lace doilies were Grandma Helen's favorite knitting project, but I decided to celebrate her with a lace shawl instead. I made my design in a soft shade of green, a color that looked beautiful on her, and used her "crocheted-off" edging—I call it "Helen's Loopy Bind-Off"—rather than a conventional knitted bind-off. I don't know whether Grandma made up the edging herself or learned it from someone, but it makes a beautiful, delicate, and flexible edging for the shawl.

SKILL LEVEL
Experienced

SIZE
One size

FINISHED MEASUREMENTS
- Width: approximately 54 inches
- Length: approximately 30 inches

MATERIALS
- Lorna's Laces Yarns Helen's Lace [50% silk / 50% wool; 1250 yd / 1140m per 4 oz skein], one skein color 43NS sage
- Stitch markers
- One 29-inch US #4 (3.5mm) circular needle
- Crochet hook size E (3.5mm)
- Waste yarn or spare needle for holding stitches not in use
- Approximately 300 size 8 seed beads
- Tapestry needle

GAUGE
20 sts and 28 rows = 4 inch in Stockinette st (blocked)

NOTES
Shawl is worked back-and-forth in one piece. A circular needle is used to accommodate the large number of stitches.

STITCH PATTERN

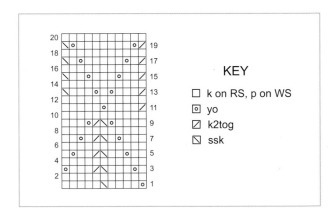

KEY
- □ k on RS, p on WS
- ⊙ yo
- ⊠ k2tog
- ◩ ssk

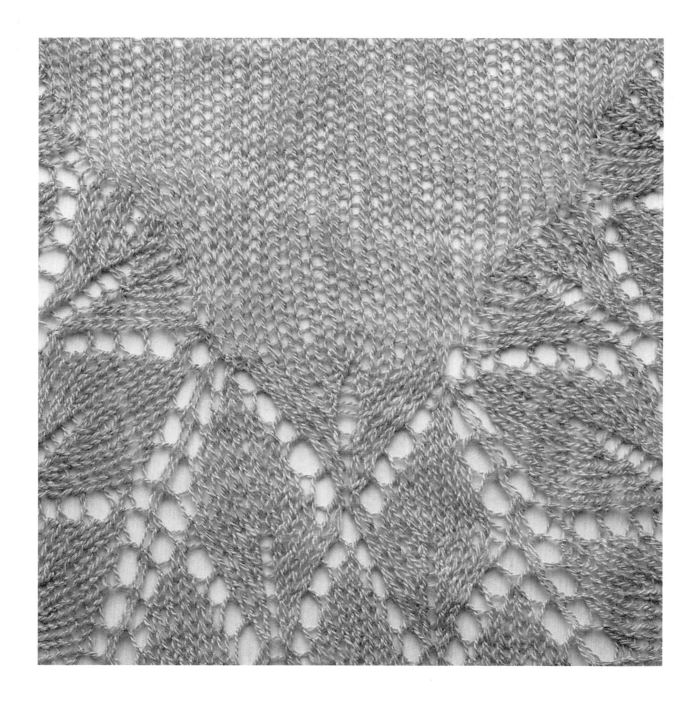

## Leaf Lace Pattern (multiple of 11)

**Rows 1 – 6:** *Knit 5, p5; repeat from *.

**Rows 7 – 12:** *Purl 5, k5; repeat from *.

**Row 1:** *Yo, k4, ssk, k5; repeat from *.

**Row 2 and all WS rows:** Purl.

**Row 3:** *K1, yo, k3, ssk, k2tog, k3, yo; repeat from *.

**Row 5:** *K2, yo, k2, ssk, k2tog, k2, yo, k1; repeat from *.

**Row 7:** *K3, yo, k1, ssk, k2tog, k1, yo, k2; repeat from *.

**Row 9:** *K4, yo, ssk, k2tog, yo, k3; repeat from *.

**Row 11:** *K2tog, k4, yo, k5; repeat from *.

**Row 13:** *K2tog, k3, yo, k1, yo, k3, ssk; repeat from * .

**Row 15:** *K2tog, k2, yo, k3, yo, k2, ssk; repeat from *.

**Row 17:** *K2tog, k1, yo, k5, yo, k1, ssk; repeat from *.

**Row 19:** *K2tog, yo, k7, yo, ssk; repeat from *.

**Row 20:** Purl.

### DIRECTIONS

Cast on 13 sts.

**Row 1:** Yo, purl across.

**Row 2:** Yo, knit across.

Repeat Rows 1 and 2 until there are 150 sts. Place all sts on a spare needle or contrasting waste yarn.

Pick up and knit 136 sts along one side of triangle, place marker, pick up and knit 1 st at corner of triangle, place marker, pick up and knit 13 sts across bottom of triangle, place marker pick up and knit 1 st at corner of triangle, place marker, pick up and knit 136 sts along side of triangle.

**WS Rows:** Knit 3, purl to last 3 sts, slipping markers, knit 3.

**RS Rows:** Knit 3, work Leaf Lace Pattern to first marker, yo, slip marker, knit 1, slip marker, yo, work Leaf Lace to next marker, yo, slip marker, knit 1, slip marker, yo, work Leaf Lace to last 3 sts, k3.

Continue these 2 rows until 4 repeats of Leaf Lace Pattern are completed. Thread all sts onto waste yarn. Cut yarn, leaving a tail of approx 20 yards. String 300 beads onto yarn.

## Bind Off

Use crochet hook instead of knitting needle for Helen's Loopy Bind-Off.

Insert hook purlwise through 3 sts together, pull loop through.

* Chain 5, push 1 bead up to hook, chain 5, insert hook purlwise through next 4 sts together, pull loop through all 5 sts (including loop on hook), chain 5, push 1 bead up to hook, chain 5, insert hook purlwise through next 3 sts together, pull loop through all 4 sts, chain 5, push 1 bead up to hook, chain 5, insert hook purlwise through next 4 sts together, pull loop through all 5 sts. Repeat from *.

At corners, adjust number of sts grouped as needed so that corner stitch is centered.

When the end of the row is reached, work as follows across the top edge of shawl:

* Chain 5, push 1 bead up to hook, chain 5, insert hook into 2nd garter st ridge (4th row) edge stitch, pull up loop, repeat from * to work across garter st edge of Leaf Lace, then across Stockinette st section *chain 5, push 1 bead up to hook, chain 5, insert hook purlwise through next 3 sts together, pull loop through all 4 sts; repeat across Stockinette section, then work remaining garter st edging same as previously.

End off. Weave in ends. Block shawl.

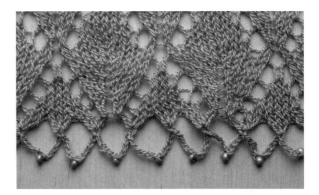

# TEARS *in* HEAVEN

I like to knit baby sweaters for many reasons. They require little planning, knit up quickly, and are relatively inexpensive to make because they use small amounts of yarn. They're also great "experiments" for adult designs but always fit, and babies never complain about color or style. Mommies always appreciate them, and love that their babies have received original gifts. I usually try to use machine-washable yarns so as not to add more work to a new mom's life. I also use yarns that are thick and cozy, rather than traditional fine baby yarns, because I love the look of a "grown-up" sweater on a baby. Every sweater is original, just as every baby is unique.

I started knitting baby sweaters in 1983, when my first son was born. In the decades since, I've knit baby sweaters for pregnant friends, friends of friends, extended family members—even the waitress at the coffee shop and the DJ for the local radio station. Sometimes friends joke that they want to get pregnant just so they will receive one of my baby sweaters. It brings me as much joy to whip up these little sweaters as it gives the recipients to dress their babies in them—possibly more.

But the truest, deepest reason I have for knitting baby sweaters is because of the baby I have in heaven. She never lived here on earth; I never got to be a mother to her, or to hold her in my arms. All the love that goes into every baby sweater is sent to heaven for my precious child. Sometimes I make so many sweaters before there are even babies to give them to that I donate them to my local crisis pregnancy center. I pray for these babies and their moms, and the sweaters are the tangible gifts of my prayers and love.

# Sweet Baby Sweater

After so many years of knitting baby sweaters, I've developed a very simple template that I can use for any yarn I stumble upon. I rarely do a gauge swatch (horrors!) because a precise fit is unnecessary for babies—they come in many sizes and always grow! This little sweater is knit in one piece up to the armholes, then divided for the left and right fronts and the back. After joining the shoulders (the only seams), each sleeve is picked up around an armhole and knit down on a circular needle. The design might look a bit challenging at first, but the stitch patterns are all combinations of knit and purl, and the sweater itself requires only a little shaping at the neck and sleeves. The front edgings can be either knit or crocheted. Once you've sewn on some cute buttons, the sweater is ready to give away.

---

## SKILL LEVEL
Intermediate

## SIZES
6 months (1 year, 2 years)

## FINISHED MEASUREMENTS
- Chest: 20 (22, 24) inches
- Length (from hem to shoulder): 10½ (12, 13½) inches

## MATERIALS
- Heirloom Breeze (30% wool / 69.6% cotton / 0.4% lycra; 104 yd per 50g skein), one (two, two) skein(s) each color
  - dark blue #006 or wine #022 [A]
  - sage green #023 or rose #005 [B]
  - light blue #007 or pink #020 [C]
- US #7 (4.5mm) knitting needles
- One 24-inch US #7 (4.5mm) circular needle
- Stitch holders
- Three ¾-inch buttons, JHB International #24041 Little Star or #22476 Muted Leaves
- Tapestry needle

## GAUGE
18 sts and 24 rows = 4 inches in seed st

## NOTES
Sweater is worked back-and-forth in one piece up to the underarms, then divided and worked separately for fronts and back. Sleeves are worked from the cuff to the shoulder, seamed and inserted into armhole. A circular needle is used to accommodate the large number of stitches, but all pieces are worked back and forth.

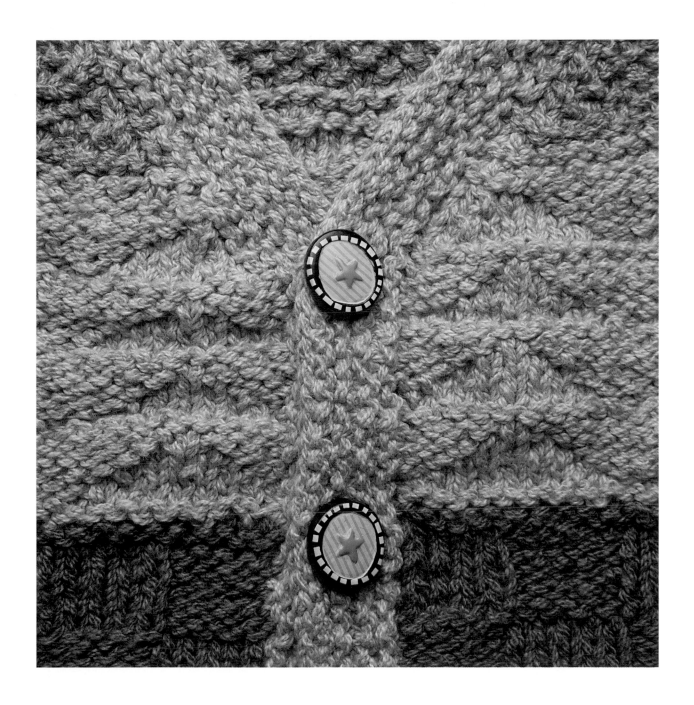

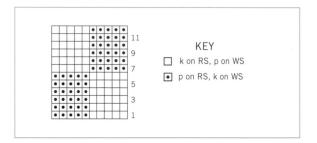

**KEY**
☐ k on RS, p on WS
⊡ p on RS, k on WS

## 5 x 5 Blocks Pattern (multiple of 10)

**Rows 1 – 6:** *Knit 5, p5; repeat from *

**Rows 7 – 12:** *Purl 5, k5; repeat from *

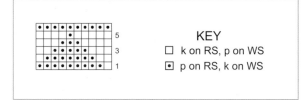

**KEY**
☐ k on RS, p on WS
⊡ p on RS, k on WS

## Triangles Pattern (multiple of 10)

**Row 1:** *Knit 1, p9; repeat from *

**Row 2:** *Purl 1, k7, p2; repeat from *

**Row 3:** *Knit 3, p5, k2; repeat from *

**Row 4:** *Purl 3, k3, p4; repeat from *

**Row 5:** *Knit 5, p1, k4; repeat from *

**Row 6:** Knit across.

## Seed Stitch (multiple of 2)

**Row 1:** *Knit 1, p1; repeat from *.

**Row 2:** Purl the knit sts and knit the purl sts.

### Body

With A and circular needle, cast on 90 (100, 110) sts. Knit 1 row (WS). Work in 5 x 5 Blocks Pattern for 3½ (4, 4½)", ending after a WS row. Knit 2 rows. Change to B and knit 2 rows. Continue in Triangles Pattern until body measures 6 (7, 8)" from cast-on edge.

### Divide for Armholes and Shape Neck

Work in pattern across 22 (25, 27) sts and place on holder for right front. Continue in pattern across next 46 (50, 56) sts for back, place remaining 22 (25, 27) sts on holder for left front.

### Upper Back

Working on back sts only, continue in pattern until back measures 7 (8, 9)" from cast-on edge, ending after a WS row. Knit 2 rows. Change to C and knit 2 rows. Continue in seed st until back measures 10½ (12, 13½)" from cast-on edge. Cut yarn, leaving sts on needle.

### Fronts

With RS facing, join B to underarm and work across left front in est pattern.

### Shape Neck

Continue working pattern to match back, decrease 1 st at neck edge every RS row 11 (12, 12) times—11 (13, 15) sts remain. Work even until front measures same length as back. Cut yarn, leaving sts on needle. Join B to underarm of right front and work to match left front.

### Join Shoulders

With right sides together, join shoulder sts using three-needle bind-off.

Holding needles parallel with right sides together, put third (right) needle through 1st stitch on front needle then through 1st stitch on back needle, knit these 2 sts together. Repeat for 2nd stitch. *Two stitches now are on right needle. Lift right-most stitch over last stitch knit and off the needle. One stitch now bound off. Knit together next stitches from front needle and back needle Repeat from * until all stitches are bound off.

### Sleeves

*Note:* Sleeve shaping occurs at the same time as color/stitch patterning. Read the instructions all the way through before you begin.

With A, cast on 25 (30, 35) sts. Knit 1 row (WS). Increase 1 st at each edge every 4th (4th, 6th) row 7 (8, 7) times, AND AT THE SAME TIME, work in 5 x 5 Blocks Pattern for 2 (2½, 2¾)", ending after a WS row. Knit 2 rows. Change to B and knit 2 rows. Continue in Triangles Pattern until sleeve measures 4 (5, 5½)" from cast-on edge. Knit 2 rows. Change to C and knit 2 rows. Work in seed st until sleeve measures 6½ (7, 8)". 39 (46, 49) sts. Bind off all sts. Sew sleeve seam. Sew sleeve into armhole opening.

### Neck Edging

With C, begin at lower right front edge and pick up approximately 47 (54, 61) sts along front edge to shoulder, knit across center 24 (24, 26) sts for back neck, pick up another 47 (54, 61) sts down left front to hem—approx 118 (132, 148) sts. Knit 3 rows.

*Buttonhole row for boy version:* On next RS row, knit to last 28 (32, 36) sts, [k2tog, yo, k10 (12, 14)] two times, k2tog, yo, k2. Knit 3 rows. Bind off all sts. Sew buttons to right front to correspond with buttonholes.

*Buttonhole row for girl version:* On next RS row, knit 2, [k2tog, yo, k10 (12, 14)] two times, k2tog, yo, knit to end of row. Knit 3 rows. Bind off all sts. Sew buttons to left front to correspond with buttonholes. Weave in ends. Block sweater.

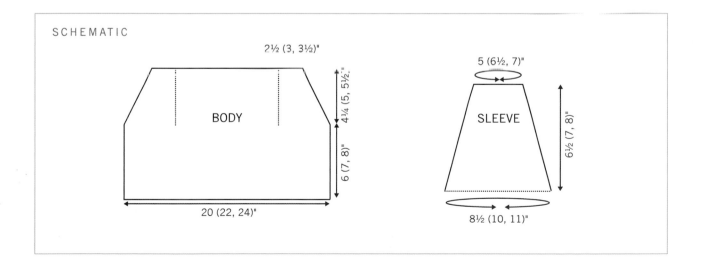

SCHEMATIC

2½ (3, 3½)"

BODY

4¼ (5, 5½)"

6 (7, 8)"

20 (22, 24)"

5 (6½, 7)"

SLEEVE

6½ (7, 8)"

8½ (10, 11)"

# CHOOSING *the*
# RIGHT MENTOR

Early in our marriage, when our son was still a toddler, we moved from the city of San Jose, California, to Placerville, a small town in the Sierra Nevada foothills. The stores were few—unless you counted the gift shops and antique stores—and all of them closed at 5:00 p.m. When you're new to a small town it can take a while to connect with people and make friends, which was especially difficult with a three-year-old toddler who spent his time sticking keys in electrical outlets, putting plastic toys on the woodstove, and having many other creative, dangerous adventures.

I had learned to knit as a child, focused on sewing as a teenager and young newlywed, then began knitting again when my son was born. His first sweater was very basic, and made from acrylic yarn I had bought at the grocery store. Not long after our move to Placerville, my son and I took a walk to the local yarn shop. I wanted to see what kinds of yarn they carried, but I was also eager to learn all I could about knitting—and to meet other knitters, too.

At the shop I met a woman named Ida, a spinning teacher who demonstrated her craft every Thursday to help attract new customers. This warm, talkative, and energetic woman, who wore Birkenstocks and lumpy handspun sweaters and socks, was remarkable to me. She was older than my mother, yet I felt an easy, comfortable kinship with her immediately. She raised sheep and llamas and angora bunnies whose wool and fur she spun into yarn, which she then dyed using plants and bugs, and she could knit without ever following a pattern. I was fascinated, and saw much that I wanted to learn from her. For her part, Ida saw bits of herself in me: a passion for fibers, colors, and creativity. She knew how to ignite that spark in me, and she did.

Over the next fifteen years, Ida taught me everything she knew about fibers. She also became a beloved friend, and a part of our growing family. When my daughter was born, it was Ida who took care of my four-year-old son.

Ida thought outside of the box, colored outside of the lines. She tried new things every day, till the day she died. With Ida's mentoring, I became a dyer and a designer. She helped set free my creativity—another of the gifts I had been given. Ida had those gifts and more, and she was a blessing to our family.

# Angora Gloves and Toy Bunny

These patterns were among Ida's favorites to knit from her handspun angora. Angora is eight times warmer than sheep's wool, and like wool, stays warm even when it gets wet. Ida made dozens of pairs of gloves as gifts. They're "fuzz-less" as they're knitted, but after a few wearings the angora blossoms, creating warm, fuzzy halos for the hands. The bunny also shows more fuzz after being given some love.

## Angora Gloves

**SKILL LEVEL**
Intermediate

**SIZE**
Adult size

**FINISHED MEASUREMENT**
Circumference: 8 inches

**MATERIALS**
- Tanglewood Fiber Creations [50% angora / 25% cashmere / 25% silk; 198 yd per 5½ oz skein], one skein color chocolate
- One set of four or five US #4 (3.5mm) double-pointed needles
- Stitch markers
- Tapestry needle

**GAUGE**
18 sts and 26 rnds = 4 inches in Stockinette st

**NOTE**
Glove fits both right and left hands; make 2.

**DIRECTIONS**
Cast on 36 sts, and divide evenly over 3 needles. Join, being careful not to twist. Work in knit 2, purl 2 ribbing for 20 rounds. Knit 8 rounds even.

**Increase for Thumb Gusset**
Place marker, increase 1, knit 1, make 1, place marker, knit to end of round.
**Round 1:** Knit one round even.
**Round 2:** Slip marker, make 1, knit to marker, make 1, slip marker, knit to end of round.
Repeat rounds 1 and 2 until there are 13 sts between the markers.
**Next round:** Knit across 13 thumb sts and slide them onto a

holder, continue to work around in Stockinette st. Cast on 1 st above thumb sts. Knit even for 1½".

## Divide for Fingers

*Index finger:* Knit 5 sts, cast on 2, knit 5–12 sts. Knit even for 2¾". Knit 2 together around. Cut yarn, leaving a 6" tail. Using tapestry needle, thread tail through remaining 6 sts.

*Middle finger:* Pick up 2 sts from cast-on sts of index finger, knit 4, cast on 3, knit 4–13 sts. Knit even for 3¼". K2tog around, end k1. Cut yarn leaving a 6" tail. Using tapestry needle, thread tail through remaining 7 sts.

*Ring finger:* Pick up 3 sts from cast-on sts of middle finger, knit 4, cast on 2, knit 4—13 sts. Knit even for 2¾". K2tog around, end k1. Cut yarn leaving a 6" tail. Using tapestry needle, thread tail through remaining 7 sts.

*Pinkie finger:* Pick up 1 st from cast-on sts of ring finger, knit 10—11 sts. Knit even for 2". K2tog around, end k1. Cut yarn leaving a 6" tail. Using tapestry needle, thread tail through remaining 6 sts.

*Thumb:* Pick up 2 sts from cast-on sts of hand, knit 13 –15 sts. Knit even for 1¾". K2tog around, end k1. Cut yarn leaving a 6" tail. Using tapestry needle, thread tail through remaining 8 sts.

Weave in ends.

# Stuffed Toy Bunny

SIZE
Approximately 12 inches tall

MATERIALS
- Tanglewood Fiber Creations [50% angora / 25% cashmere / 25% silk; 198 yd per 5½ oz skein], one skein color silver
- One set of four or five US #9 (5.5mm) double-pointed needles
- Stuffing
- Ribbon, one-half yard
- Yarn or embroidery floss for face
- Tapestry needle

GAUGE
3 sts and 4 rows = 1 inch in Stockinette st

NOTE
Bunny is knit in the round in one piece. Embroidered or stitched lines define the neck and extremities after the bunny is stuffed.

DIRECTIONS
Cast on 20 sts, and divide over 3 needles. Join, being careful not to twist. Knit every round for 4".

**Arms**
Cast on 12 sts at beginning of round, knit 10, cast on 12 sts, knit last 10 sts of round—44 sts. Knit every round for 2". Bind off 12 sts, knit 10, bind off 12 sts, knit last 10 sts.

**Head**
Knit every round for 2".

**Ears**
Knit 5 sts, turn. Purl 10, turn. Knit 10. Work back and forth on these 10 sts only in Stockinette st for 3". Next RS row: K2tog. Cut yarn, leaving a 12" tail and thread through remaining 5 sts. Join yarn and work second ear in same manner. Sew all openings except at the bottom.

Stuff bunny to desired firmness. Using yarn, backstitch lines to divide legs, neck, ears, and arms. Tie ribbon around neck. Embroider face.

# KNITTING TOGETHER
## *a* FRIENDSHIP

By the time my daughter was born, my friend (and expert spinner) Ida had opened my eyes to exciting possibilities in knitting and yarns. I couldn't wait to knit pink things and spin fluffy wool from our angora bunnies into warm cuddlies for my baby girl—my little "dolly"—to wear. The small country church we had just joined embraced our family with love by sending us home-cooked meals and throwing a baby shower. Three baby girls had all been born into our community in the same week, so the church ladies threw a triple baby girl shower. I didn't know the other mothers at all, but I felt that I should bring gifts for their babies. Naturally I had been busy, so I thought about what I could make quickly. I played with simple knitted squares of handspun angora, adding a row of eyelets that I threaded with a pretty ribbon to make warm, fuzzy baby booties.

The other mothers—both new moms—appreciated the booties, which were so soft and stayed on so well. One of the women, Judy, surprised me with her enthusiasm. She was so inspired by my gift that she immediately wanted to spin and dye yarn and knit. Once I introduced Judy to Ida, she dove headfirst into learning about all aspects of fiber. Soon we were meeting several times a week so that we could spin or knit while our babies played together. Judy and I swapped angora bunnies so we could increase our "herds" of colorful wool, and eventually bought a small flock of sheep. We began hosting "Wool Gatherings," big parties where dozens of local fiber artists would sell their handmade soaps, sweaters, yarn, bunnies and sheep, fleeces, spinning wheels, plants and more.

Eventually Judy and I ran a small business selling our handknit sweaters, handspun yarns, and knitting and spinning supplies. We sold our creations at local craft shows, taking turns running the booth and looking after the two girls. Our two little blondes remained friends well past the days of our business relationship.

These are the baby booties that started it all.

# Friendship Booties

For this project you'll need about 40 yards of bulky-weight angora-blend wool, ideally handspun, which doesn't shed as easily as commercial yarn. The beauty of these booties is their simplicity—they are basically a rectangle, making them quick and easy to finish. The pretty ribbons, soft against the baby's skin, tie around the ankles to keep them securely in place.

## SKILL LEVEL
Easy

## SIZE
Newborn

## FINISHED MEASUREMENT
Length: approximately 3 inches

## MATERIALS
- Tanglewood Fiber Creations [50% wool 50% angora; 60 yd/55m per 50g skein], one skein color natural white
- Smooth cotton waste yarn, three yards
- US #9 (5.5mm) knitting needles
- ³⁄₈-inch wide ribbon, one yard
- Tapestry needle

## GAUGE
3 sts and 4 rows = 1 inch in Stockinette st

## DIRECTIONS

Cast on 16 sts using waste yarn. (This will be removed later.) Join working yarn, leaving a 36" tail at beginning of row.

**Row 1:** Purl.

**Row 2:** K2tog, yo, knit to last 2 sts, yo, ssk.

Repeat these 2 rows 9 more times.

K2tog across. Cut yarn, leaving a 12" tail. Using tapestry needle, thread yarn through remaining 8 sts. Pull tight and fasten off yarn.

Remove waste yarn from cast-on edge. Put stitches onto needle. P2tog across row. Using tapestry needle, thread yarn through remaining 8 sts. Pull tight and fasten off yarn.

Bootie will now look like a little canoe with eyelets across the top edges. Cut ribbon to 24" length. Weave in and out of eyelets, beginning at either end. Bootie will bunch around baby's foot and tie on snuggly around the ankle.

# WHEN *a* FRIEND's
# FAITH *is* GREATER

Shanna owned Placerville Yarn, one of the largest, best-stocked, and most interesting yarn shops in northern California. She believed in offering unique products and supporting local businesses. When I first started dyeing yarns, I would simply dye up bundles and bring them to her shop for her to sell. Hand-dyed yarns were uncommon back then, so they sold very quickly.

In her customers' enthusiasm for my yarns, Shanna saw great potential for community interaction. She organized a fashion show at Town Hall. She and I designed every garment, and every garment used my yarns—the first Lorna's Laces. The attendance was huge, the catering was perfect, and the fashion show was a hit.

Her next step was to encourage me to sell my yarns to other stores. At that time I really didn't understand how the industry worked, or to whom I should talk. When one of her yarn sales representatives came to town, she arranged a meeting between us. She was willing to give up exclusivity so that I could build my business; she saw that its potential was far greater than I could envision. I'm still grateful for her generous encouragement, and amazed at the faith she had in me.

# Shanna's Cable and Lace Vest

I've tried to design a garment that reflects Shanna's feminine, tasteful style, and acknowledges her love of texture, cables, and lace. Consequently, this is a very advanced project, because the cables, lace, and shaping must all be done simultaneously. Shanna also loves working with finer-gauge yarns on smaller needles, and the yarn featured in this vest is still one of her favorites.

SKILL LEVEL
Experienced

SIZES
Fitted sizes, per measurements below

FINISHED MEASUREMENTS
- Bust: 34 (37, 40, 44, 47) inches
- Length (hem to back neck):
  21½ (22½, 23½, 24½, 25½) inches

MATERIALS
- Lorna's Laces Shepherd Sport (100% superwash wool, 200 yd per 2.6 oz skein), four (four, five, five, six) skeins color Manzanita #2ns
- US #4 (3.5 mm) knitting needles
- One 16-inch US #4 (3.5 mm) circular needle
- Stitch markers
- Stitch holders
- Cable needle
- Tapestry needle

GAUGE
24 sts and 30 rows = 4 inches in Floral Lace Pattern

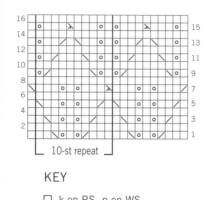

KEY

☐ k on RS, p on WS
☑ yo
☑ k2tog
☑ ssk
☑ sl 1 knitwise, k2tog, psso

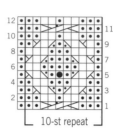

L— 10-st repeat —J

KEY

☐ knit
☑ purl
◉ (k1, yo, k1) into st, turn, p3, turn, k3, turn, p3, turn, k3tog
☑ 2CL: sl next 2 sts to cn and hold in front, p1, k2 from cn
☑ 2CR: sl next st to cn and hold in back, k2, p1 from cn
☑ sl 3 to cn and hold in back, k2, (p1, k2) from cn

## Floral Lace Pattern (multiple of 10 + 1)

**Row 1:** *Knit 3, k2tog, yo, k1, yo, ssk, k2; repeat from *, end k1.

**Row 2 and all WS rows:** Purl.

**Row 3:** *Knit 2, k2tog, k1, yo, k1, yo, k1, ssk, k1; repeat from *, end k1.

**Row 5:** *Knit 1, k2tog, k2, yo, k1, yo, k2, ssk; repeat from *,end k1.

**Row 7:** K2tog, k3, yo, k1, yo, k3, *slip 1 knitwise, k2tog, psso, k3, yo, k1, yo, k3; repeat from *, end ssk.

**Row 9:** *Knit 1, yo, ssk, k5, k2tog, yo; repeat from *, end k1.

**Row 11:** Knit 1, yo, k1, ssk, k3, k2tog, k1, yo; repeat from *, end k1.

**Row 13:** *Knit 1, yo, k2, ssk, k1, k2tog, k2, yo; repeat from *, end k1.

**Row 15:** *Knit 1, yo, k3, slip 1, k2tog, psso, k3, yo; repeat from *, end k1.

**Row 16:** Purl.

## Bobbled Cable Edging (multiple of 10 + 1)

**Row 1 (RS):** Purl 1,* p2, slip 3 sts to cable needle and hold in back, k2, then p1, k2 from cable needle, p3; repeat from *.

**Row 2:** *K3, p2, k1, p2, k2; repeat from *, end k1.

**Row 3:** *P2, 2CR, p1, 2CL, p1; repeat from *, end p1.

**Row 4:** *K2, p2, k3, p2, k1; repeat from *, end k1.

**Row 5:** *P1, 2CR, p1, make bobble, p1, 2CL; repeat from *, end p1.

**Row 6:** *K1, p2, k5, p2; repeat from *, end k1.

**Row 7:** *P1, 2CL, p3, 2CR; repeat from *, end p1.

**Row 8:** K1, *k1, p2, k3, p2, k2; repeat from *.

**Row 9:** *P2, 2CL, p1, 2CR, p1; repeat from *, end p1.

**Row 10:** Repeat Row 2.

**Row 11:** Repeat Row 1.

**Row 12:** Repeat Row 2.

**2CR** = slip 1 st to cable needle and hold in back, k2, p1 from cable needle

**2CL** = slip 2 sts to cable needle and hold in front, p1, k2 from cable needle

**Make bobble**: (k1, yo, k1) into next st, turn, p3, turn, k3, turn, p3, turn, k3tog.

## NOTES

Cable edging is worked first, then lace pattern begins in the middle of the row, working progressively longer rows to make a gently shaped, short-rowed hemline. Because the cable edging pulls in more than the lace pattern, more sts are cast on for the hem than are decreased when beginning the lace.

When working neck and armhole shapings in lace, if there aren't enough stitches for a complete or half pattern repeat, work extra stitches in Stockinette.

## DIRECTIONS

### Back

Cast on 121 (131, 141, 151, 161) sts. Knit 4 rows, ending after a WS row. Work 12 rows of Bobbled Cable Edging. Knit 3 rows. Knit next row, decreasing 18 sts across as follows: Knit 8 (5, 10, 7, 11), *k2tog, k 4 (5, 5, 6, 6); repeat 18 times, knit to end–103 (113, 123, 133, 143) sts.

Begin short rows by knitting across 62 (72, 82, 92, 102) sts, place marker, turn work and purl 21 (31, 21, 31, 41) sts, place marker and turn work.

Begin Floral Lace Pattern by working Row 1 across the marked center sts, remove marker, knit 5 sts, replace marker, turn work. Purl to marker, remove marker, purl 5, replace marker, turn work. *Work next row of Floral Lace Pattern to marker, remove marker, knit 5 sts, replace marker, turn work. Purl to marker, remove marker, purl 5, replace marker, turn work. Repeat from * until all sts are being worked in pattern, maintaining 1 st on each edge in Stockinette st (edge sts not included in chart). Remove markers. Continue even in pattern until body measures 13½ (14, 14½, 15, 15½)" at side edges.

### Shape Armholes

At beginning of next 2 rows, bind off 6 (7, 8, 9, 10) sts. Continue in pattern while decreasing 1 st at each edge every RS row 6 (7, 8, 9, 10) times–79 (85, 91, 97, 103) sts remain. Work even until armhole measures 7½ (8, 8½, 9, 9½)" from bind-off.

### Shape Shoulders

Next RS row, work in pattern to last 5 sts, turn work. Purl to last 5 sts, turn work.

Work in pattern to last 10 sts, turn work. Purl to last 10 sts, turn work. Work in pattern to last 15 sts, turn work. Purl to last 15 sts, turn work. Work in pattern to last 20 sts, turn work. Purl to last 20 sts, turn work. Work in pattern to end of row. Turn, purl to end of row. Place 21 (24, 27, 27, 30) sts from each end onto holders for shoulders. Place center 37 (37, 37, 43, 43) sts onto a holder for back neck.

### Front

Work same as back to beginning of armholes.

### Shape Neck and Armholes

Next RS row, bind off 6 (7, 8, 9, 10) sts for armhole, work in pattern to center st. Place center st on holder. Join 2nd ball of yarn and continue across remaining sts. Bind off 6 (7, 8, 9, 10) sts for armhole, purl across each upper front using separate balls of yarn. There should be 45 (49, 53, 57, 61) sts for each upper front at this point. Continue working armhole decreases as for back AND AT THE SAME TIME, decrease 1 st at each neck edge every 4th row 9 (9, 9, 11, 11) times, then every RS row 9 (9, 9, 10, 10) times. Work even on 21 (24, 27, 27, 30) sts until front measures same as back to shoulders.

*Shape Shoulders*

Beginning at neck edge, work across shoulder to last 5 sts, turn work. Work back to neck edge. Work across shoulder to last 10 sts, turn work. Work back to neck edge. Work across shoulder to last 15 sts, turn work. Work back to neck edge. Work across shoulder to last 20 sts, turn work. Work back to neck edge. Work across all sts. Return back shoulder sts to needles to join shoulders to front.

*Three-Needle Bind-Off Shoulder Join:* Holding front and back right sides together, work 3-needle bind-off: Put right needle through 1st stitch on front needle then through 1st stitch on back needle, knit as usual. Repeat for 2nd stitch. Two stitches now are on right needle. Lift right-most stitch over last stitch knit and off the needle. One stitch now bound off. Repeat across each shoulder.

## Neck Edging

Using circular needle, join yarn and knit across back neck sts. Continuing down left neck edge, pick up and knit 45 (48, 52, 54, 56) sts, knit center st from holder and place marker through it, pick up and knit 45 (48, 52, 54, 56) sts along right neck edge. Purl one round. Knit next round working double decrease at center front as follows: Knit to 1 st before marked st, slip next 2 sts together knitwise, knit next st, pass slipped sts over. Repeat these two rounds. Bind off.

Sew side seams.

## Armhole Edgings

Using circular needle, pick up and knit approximately 90 (96, 104, 108, 112) sts evenly around armhole. Purl one round. Knit one round. Repeat these 2 rounds. Bind off. Weave in ends. Block vest.

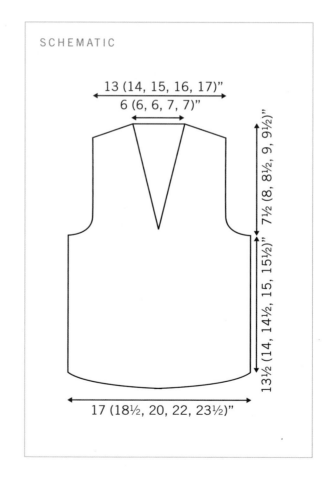

SCHEMATIC

13 (14, 15, 16, 17)"
6 (6, 6, 7, 7)"
7½ (8, 8½, 9, 9½)"
13½ (14, 14½, 15, 15½)"
17 (18½, 20, 22, 23½)"

# By
## FAITH ALONE

After a few seasons of selling my hand-dyed, handspun yarns and the garments I had made from them at local craft shows, where I just sat and hoped for sales, I was ready for a change. I had toddlers to mother, and babysitters were hard to find—and afford. When I decided to stop going to the shows, friends questioned my wisdom. "How can you sell anything staying at home?" I didn't have the answer, but I trusted that God would honor my intention to stay home with my children, and bless my next venture, whatever it would be.

He did. First, my hand-dyed yarn business took off. Within a month, my friend Shanna introduced me to a yarn representative named Jim, who gave me wise advice and opened doors for me. After helping me arrange my yarns into something presentable, he sold them to shops up and down the West Coast. I also gave Jim a few samples of slippers with suede soles that I had designed and sewn. Both my yarns and my slippers were so well received by his customers that I soon needed help—which is how His blessing spread to someone else who wished to work from home.

My neighbor, Lori, had been commuting "down the hill" as we say, in a solid hour of traffic, from our country neighborhood in Somerset to Sacramento. I knew Lori was an excellent seamstress—and a perfectionist. She took over the suede portion of my business, eventually developing it into her own: Somerset Designs. Her suede slipper soles, purse bottoms, and purse handles are still perfect, and still keep her out in the country.

# Comfy Suede-soled Slippers

When I first started selling slippers, I designed a very basic pattern to knit them. Today the slippers can be purchased finished or as kits consisting of suede soles, yarn, and my original pattern. Since Lori's business has expanded to include suede products in many pretty colors, I decided to feature one of those colors in my design. I developed the slipper pattern into something a bit more stylish, too.

---

**SKILL LEVEL**
Intermediate

**SIZE**
Sized to fit eleven sizes from babies to adults

**FINISHED MEASUREMENTS**
Length (foot): 4 (5, 6, 7, 8) 9 (9½, 10, 10½, 11, 12) inches

**MATERIALS**
- Brown Sheep Lamb's Pride [85% wool / 25% mohair; 190 yd/205m per 100g skein], one skein each color
  - Wild Violet M-173 [MC]
  - Pine Shadows M-170 [CC]
- Somerset Designs suede slipper soles, Forest
- One set of four or five US #7 (4.5 mm) double-pointed needles
- Stitch markers
- Tapestry needle

**GAUGE**
16 sts and 20 rnds = 4 inches in Slipped Stitch Pattern

## NOTES

Keep CC floats very loose so that the stitches do not pucker or distort.

Leg portion is worked in the round. Because the slipper soles have a wonderful cushioned fleece lining, to only the top of the slipper foot (instep) is knitted. After heel turn and gussets are completed, slipper top is worked back and forth to toe.

The slippers are written in eleven sizes, to match the eleven sizes produced by Somerset Designs. Measure the favored foot from heel to toe to determine the proper size in inches.

## STITCH PATTERN

### KEY
- ☐ knit
- ⊡ purl
- ☑ sl as to purl with yarn in front

### Slipped Stitch Pattern
### (multiple of 4, worked in the round)

**Round 1:** With CC, slip all sts as if to purl and with yarn in front: *Knit 1, slip 3; repeat from *.

**Round 2:** With CC, slip all sts as if to purl and with yarn in back: *Purl 1, slip 3; repeat from *.

**Round 3:** * With MC, k2, slide right needle tip under float from Round 1 and knit it tog with next st, k1; repeat from *.

**Rounds 4–6:** With MC, knit.

## DIRECTIONS

With MC, cast on 24 (24, 28, 28, 32) 36 (36, 40, 40, 44, 44) sts. Divide over 3 double-pointed needles and join, being careful not to twist. Place marker for beginning of round. Work around in knit 1, purl 1 ribbing for 5 rounds.

Change to Slipped Stitch Pattern, joining CC, and work even until leg measures 3 (3, 4, 4, 4) 5 (5, 5, 5, 6, 6)" from cast-on edge. Cut CC.

## Work Heel

With MC, knit across first 12 (12, 14, 14, 16) 18 (18, 20, 20, 22, 22) sts. Turn and purl back. Work back and forth in Stockinette st on these sts only for 8 (9, 10, 11, 12) 12 (13, 13, 13, 14, 14) rows. Bind off heel sts on next RS row but do not break yarn.

## Instep and Gussets

Pick up and knit 8 (9, 10, 11, 12) 12 (13, 13, 13, 14, 14) sts along side of heel, place marker, knit across 12 (12, 14, 14, 16) 18 (18, 20, 20, 22, 22) sts across top of foot, place marker, pick up and knit 8 (9, 10, 11, 12) 12 (13, 13, 13, 14, 14) sts along side of heel. *Turn and purl across. RS rows: Knit to 2 sts before marker, k2tog, slip marker, knit to next marker, slip marker, ssk, knit to end. Repeat from * until only 1 st remains outside of markers. Remove markers and continue even in Stockinette st until length of foot from back of heel to toe measures 3 (4, 4, 5, 6) 7 (7, 7, 7½, 8, 9)". Bind off 4 sts at beginning of next 2 rows. Bind off remaining sts.

## Assembly

Weave in ends. Pin slipper top to inside of suede soles. Sew in place using embroidery thread or sock yarn.

# INSTANT FRIEND:
# JUST Add WATER

Michele was a knitting designer who published her patterns under the name Effectiveness By Design. I was a yarn company owner. We met at a wholesale trade show and both felt an immediate connection, sort of the friendship equivalent of love at first sight. She initially approached me with the idea of dyeing a Christmas-themed yarn for a design she had planned. Within weeks I created the color, which remains a classic in the Lorna's Laces line. We each realized that our skills and gifts complemented the other's, so we knew could help each other. "Win-win" was one of Michele's favorite phrases.

Michele and I decided that we would share a hotel room when we attended trade shows. We laughed about my frequent "good fortune" at getting a free night's stay or a lobster dinner because the hotel had no hot water, or some other oversight or mistake. Michele taught me some Yiddish while she told me silly stories, and I gave her a nickname: Michele Wanelle Wyman. Having her first name misspelled was a constant annoyance, so when I booked our hotel room for a show in Seattle, I wanted to be clear about the correct spelling. "Michele with one el," I declared. When we arrived, they had booked the room for Lorna Miser and Michelle Wanelle, exactly as I had said!

Before long Michele and I became much more than business associates, we became friends. Our friendship was so immediate, so pure and natural, that no efforts (or ingredients) were necessary to make it flourish. We talked about our ideas, family issues, goals, and challenges. We tested, encouraged, and played devil's advocate for each other. We shared our hearts, worked on life together, and became like sisters. We also shared love, faith, pain, and, in the end, Michele's breast cancer.

Some family you're born into; other family adopts you and makes you feel whole. Michele will always be my big sister. She challenged me to be a stronger, more loving, and smarter person. I can't imagine my life without her influence.

# Michele's Southwestern-motif Sweater

Michele's design style was distinctive. She loved living in Arizona, and the southwest style influenced her work. Her designs often seem more difficult to knit than they really are. Her pattern instructions are incredibly detailed, and written for a wide range of sizes. There's a comfortable "wearability" to Michele's style of sweater. My sweater follows many of Michele's design approaches: it's knit seamlessly, it's fun and interesting to knit (while appearing to require more skill than it actually does), and the colors and design are reminiscent of her life in Arizona.

---

SKILL LEVEL
Experienced

SIZES
Women's XS (S, M, L) [1X, 2X, 3X].

FINISHED MEASUREMENTS
- Chest: 36 (40, 44, 48) [52, 56, 60] inches
- Length (total body): 23 (24, 25, 26) [27, 28, 29] inches

MATERIALS
- Lorna's Laces Shepherd Worsted [100% superwash wool; 225 yd/205m per 4 oz skein];
  - one (one, one, one)[two, two, two] skeins Glenwood #105 [MC]
  - one skein Grapevine #3ns [CC1]
  - one skein Poppy #50ns [CC2]
  - one skein Turquoise #22ns [CC3]

- One 16-inch US #7 (4.5mm) circular needle
- One 29-inch US #7 (4.5mm) circular needle
- One set of four or five US #7 (4.5 mm) double-pointed needles
- Stitch markers
- Stitch holders
- Cable needle
- Tapestry needle

GAUGE
18 sts and 24 rnds = 4 inches in Stockinette st

NOTES
Sweater body and sleeves are knit in the round, separately up to the underarm, then all are joined and worked seamlessly to neck.

One stitch marker should be a unique color to indicate beginning of the round.

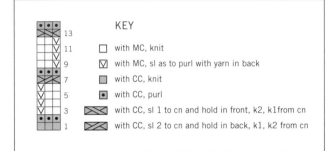

## Chandler Arizona Stitch Pattern
## (multiple of 3, worked in the round)

**Round 1:** With CC, knit.

**Round 2:** With CC, purl.

**Round 3-6:** With MC, *knit 2, slip 1; repeat from * around.

**Round 7:** With CC, *slip next 2 sts to cable needle, hold in
   back of work, k1, k2 from cable needle; repeat from *
   around.

**Round 8:** With CC, purl.

**Round 9-12:** With MC, *slip 1, knit 2; repeat from * around.

**Round 13:** With CC, *slip next st to cable needle, hold in
   front of work, k2, k1 from cable needle; repeat from *
   around.

**Round 14:** With CC, purl.

## Body

With longer circular needle and CC1, cast on 162 (180, 198,
   216) [234, 252, 270] sts. Join, being careful not to twist.
   Place marker for beginning of round.

Work rnds 1-14 of Chandler Arizona St using CC1 as CC.
   Cut CC1.

Using CC2 as CC, rep rnds 1-14. Cut CC2.

Using CC3 as CC, rep rnds 1-14 once more. Cut CC3.

**Next rnd:** With MC, k 81 (90, 99,108) [117, 126, 135] sts,
   place marker to indicate right underarm, knit to end of rnd.

Work even in Stockinette st until body measures 14½ (15,
   15½, 15½) [15½, 15½, 15½]".

### Divide for Underarm

Knit to 5 (5, 5, 6) [6, 6, 6] sts past marker, slip last
10 (10, 10, 12) [12, 12, 12] sts worked onto a stitch holder,
removing marker; knit to 5 (5, 5, 6) [6, 6, 6] sts before
end-of-rnd marker, slip next 10 (10, 10, 12) [12, 12, 12]
sts worked onto a stitch holder, removing marker. Do not cut
yarn. Leaving sts on needle, set aside body.

### Sleeves

With double-pointed needles and CC1, cast on 51 (51, 54,
57) [63, 63, 66] sts. Join, being careful not to twist. Place
marker for beginning of round. Work 42 rnds of Chandler
Arizona St as for body using colors as est. Next rnd: With
MC, knit, increasing 7 (9, 10, 11) [13, 15, 16] sts evenly
spaced—58 (60, 64, 68) [76, 78, 82] sts. Continue in
Stockinette st, increasing at beginning and end of round
every 8th round 4 (4, 5, 5) [5, 6, 7] times and changing to
16" circular when there are enough sts. Work even on
66 (68,74, 78) [86, 90, 96] sts until sleeve measures
17½ (17½, 18, 18) [18½, 18½, 19]" or about 1" shorter
than desired sleeve length.  Next rnd: Knit to  5 (5, 5, 6)
[6, 6, 6] sts before marker, place next 10 (10, 10, 12) [12,
12, 12] sts on holder. Cut yarn and place remaining 56 (58,
64, 66, 74, 78, 84) sts on separate holder. Set aside. Make
another sleeve, leaving last 56 (58, 64, 66, 74, 78, 84) sts
on needles.

## Join for Yoke

Using longer circular needle and continuing with MC yarn attached to body sts, knit 56 (58, 64, 66, 74, 78, 84) sleeve sts for left sleeve, place marker, knit 71 (80, 89, 96) [105, 114, 123] front sts, place marker, knit 56 (58, 64, 66, 74, 78, 84) sts from holder for right sleeve, place marker, knit across remaining 71 (80, 89, 96) [105, 114, 123] back sts, place unique color marker for end of round—254 (276, 306, 324) [358, 384, 414] sts. Knit 4 (2, 0, 0) [0, 0, 0] rnds even. Decrease Round: *K1, ssk, knit to 3 sts before marker, k2tog, k1; repeat from * 3 more times. Knit 1 round even. Work these 2 rnds 15 (17, 19, 20) [24, 26, 29] more times–126 (132, 146, 156) [158, 168, 174] sts remain.

## Shape Neck

Mark 9 (14, 11, 16) [17, 18, 21] center front stitches for neck. Next rnd: Knit to first center front marker, remove marker, place next 9 (14, 11, 16) [17,18, 21] sts on holder, remove marker, knit around to beg of neck edge—117 (118, 135, 140) [141, 150, 153] sts. Turn. Purl 1 row. Decrease Row: K1, k2tog, *knit to 3 sts from next marker, k2tog, k1, slip marker, k1, ssk; repeat from * 3 times, knit to last 3 sts, ssk, k1. Purl 1 row. Repeat these 2 rows 4 (4, 6, 6) [6, 7, 7] more times—67 (68, 65, 70) [71, 70, 73] sts. Last row: K1, k2tog, k1, * slip marker, k1, ssk, knit to 3 sts from marker, k2tog, k1; repeat from * 3 times, slip marker, k1, ssk, k1–51 (52, 49, 54) [55, 54, 57] sts.

## Neck Edging

ith shorter circular needle and MC, pick up 9 (9, 11, 11) [11, 13, 13] sts from left neck edge, knit across 9 (14, 11, 16) [17, 18, 21] sts from front neck stitch holder, pick up 9 (9, 11, 11) [11, 13, 13] sts from right neck edge, knit around neck sts—78 (84, 82, 92) [94, 98, 104] sts. Purl 1 round, knit 1 round, purl 1 round. Bind off loosely.

Graft underarm sts using kitchener stitch. Weave in ends. Block sweater.

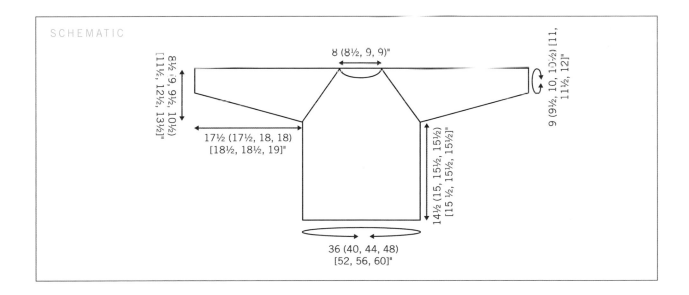

SCHEMATIC

8½ (9, 9½, 10½) [11¼, 12½, 13½]"

8 (8½, 9, 9)"

9 (9½, 10, 10½) [11, 11½, 12]"

17½ (17½, 18, 18) [18½, 18½, 19]"

14½ (15, 15½, 15½) [15 ½, 15½, 15½]"

36 (40, 44, 48) [52, 56, 60]"

# Two SOFT HEARTS BECOME One

Although exhibiting at trade shows can be stressful, I've managed to make many friends while attending them. During one show, when there were just a few people left on the show floor at the end of the day, a beautiful yarn shop owner came into my booth to place an order for yarns and kits. She was warm and friendly, and as we talked we began to grow comfortable with each other and enjoyed sharing bits of our personal lives.

We spoke at a leisurely pace, meandering from choosing yarn to making purchasing decisions to having difficulty making decisions. And when this beautiful woman felt safe with me, she shared her heart openly, trusting that I would listen and empathize. She poured out her heart to me, and my heart broke with the thought of the pain that she was carrying. We sat on the floor behind one of my displays racks, hugging and weeping.

What a privilege that she trusted me with her story and her tears! We hardly knew each other, yet at that moment I was there to fill a need—as her friend. I continue to see her at trade shows, and although we never talk about that tender connection, I know that it gave us a foundation of trust and compassion. She is definitely in a happier chapter of her life now. I look forward to having lighter conversations with her, but I just might pour out my heart to her the next time I see her.

# Heart Pillow

This incredibly soft, luxurious pillow is my tribute to the day that two women—both yarn industry professionals—met and shared their hearts. The silk of the yarn and the beads that embellish it are precious, but the time spent with someone who cares about your heart is priceless.

SKILL LEVEL
Experienced

SIZE
One Size

FINISHED MEASUREMENTS
* Width: approximately 14 inches
* Height: approximately 12 inches

MATERIALS
* ArtYarns Silk Rhapsody [50% silk / 50% kid mohair; 260 yd/238m per 100g skein], one skein color RH130 [A]
* ArtYarns Beaded Silk [100% silk with glass beads; 100 yd/91m per 50g skein], one skein color BS130G [B]
* Stitch markers
* One pair of four or five US #6 (4mm) double-pointed needles
* One 32-inch US #7 (4.5mm) circular needle
* Point protector
* Half-pound bag of polyfill
* Tapestry needle

GAUGE
20 sts and 48 rows = 4 inches in garter st with A

NOTES
Work increases by knitting into front and back of same stitch. Make two hearts, pin or baste them together, then attach them by picking up a stitch along the edge through both hearts and working beaded lace edging around.

## DIRECTIONS

### Hearts (make 2 for each pillow)

With A and circular needle, cast on 50 sts, place marker, cast
on 50 sts. Mark next row as RS.

**RS Rows:** Increase, knit to 2 sts before marker, ssk, slip
marker, k2tog, knit to last st, inc.

**WS Rows:** Knit.

Work these 2 rows until 26 rows (13 ridges) have been
worked.

**RS Rows:** Knit to 2 sts before marker, ssk, slip marker, k2tog,
knit to end.

**WS Rows:** Knit.

Work these 2 rows until 12 rows (6 ridges) have been worked.

**RS Rows:** Ssk, knit to 2 sts before marker, ssk, slip marker,
k2tog, knit to last 2 sts, k2tog.

**WS Rows:** Knit.

Work these 2 rows until 12 rows (6 ridges) have been worked.

**RS Rows:** Ssk, k2tog, knit to 2 sts before marker, ssk, slip
marker, k2tog, knit to last 4 sts, ssk, k2tog.

**WS Rows:** Knit.

Work these 2 rows until 10 rows (5 ridges) have been worked.
Bind off remaining sts.

### Edging

*Note:* Stitches are picked up all around the pillow starting
at the top center of the heart. Edging is knit sideways and
attached to the pillow at the end of every WS row while
working clockwise around the pillow. When working the
"p2tog" with the last st and the heart edge, it may be easier
to maneuver by sliding the last st from left needle over to
the needle holding the heart edge sts, then purling these
2 together.

Holding 2 hearts wrong sides together, whipstitch edges

together, leaving a 3" opening. With A and circular needle,
pick up sts around all edges as follows: Along the opening,
pick up through the top layer of pillow only, and around the
remainder of the pillow, through both layers. Stitches should
be picked up at a rate of 1 stitch in every other stitch on
cast-on and bound-off edges and 1 stitch for every other row
(one per ridge) on side edges—approx 126 sts total. Leave
these sts on circular needle and put needle protector on one
end. Cut yarn.

With B and double-pointed needles, cast on 6 sts.

Purl 5 sts, then p2tog using last st on left needle and 1st st
from heart edge. Turn work—6 sts.

**Row 1:** K1, yo, k2tog, yo, k2tog, yo, k1—7 sts.

**Row 2:** Purl 6 sts, then p2tog using last st on left needle and
next st from heart edge.

**Row 3:** K1, yo, k2tog, yo, k2tog, yo, k2—8 sts.

**Row 4:** Purl 7 sts, then p2tog using last st on left needle and
next st from heart edge.

**Row 5:** K1, yo, k2tog, yo, k2tog, yo, k3—9 sts.

**Row 6:** Bind off 3, p4, p2tog using last st on left needle and
next st from heart edge.

Continue around heart until all sts are used. Bind off all sts.
Join bound-off sts to cast-on sts. Stuff pillow. Sew opening
closed. Weave in ends

### Beaded Heart Edging Chart

KEY

☐ k on RS, p on WS

⊙ yo

☑ k2tog on RS, p2tog on WS

▬ bind off

# A BUSINESS *is* BLESSED
## ... *and* BLESSES

September 11th dealt a serious blow to the country, and left every last one of my friends shaken, too. We didn't know anyone personally who had died, but the horror of that day made us want to do something to help those who had been affected directly. When I was finally able to stop crying and pull myself away from the television a couple of days later, I went for a quiet walk to think about how I could lend a hand and show my patriotism. I wanted to do something that was somehow productive and made things feel "normal" again.

On my walk I thought about how I had once considered dyeing a sock yarn in a red, white, and blue colorway and naming it "Americana." This was the perfect time to do it. Creating the color was simple. One of my employees suggested changing the name to "Liberty" and giving it the number "1776" instead of following our systematic numbering plan for identifying colors. Both were clever ideas that stuck. But once my patriotic yarn was in the works, I needed to figure out how I could best use it to support the country and the victims of 9/11.

At the time I belonged to an online sock-knitting group whose enthusiastic members buy more yarn than they can ever knit, and shared my idea with them. After listening to some suggestions, I decided to dedicate the net profits of all sales to the Salvation Army, and to temporarily sell the yarn directly to knitters to increase the profit margin.

Upon its release, Liberty Shepherd Sock Yarn became a record-breaking hit. Later, yarn shops ordered it by the hundreds of skeins. My staff was completely overwhelmed by having to keep up with those orders while taking care of our regular orders at the same time, so I decided to approach my church and ask for help. I hosted several yarn parties, complete with brownies and lemonade, where even my non-knitting friends pitched in to twist, label, bag, and ship hundreds of pounds of yarn.

Everyone benefited from those days. Knitters were able to buy a product they enjoyed and support a great charity. My friends got to take part in a big project that allowed them to contribute to a great cause and begin healing by talking about the world's events. I felt blessed because knitters, shop owners, and friends all supported my idea, and allowed me to do something to come to terms with my own sadness.

# Ladies Liberty Socks

Because socks are such a popular knitting project, knitters everywhere were knitting their favorite sock pattern in "liberty" colors after September 11. I like to mix up hand-dyed colors using slipped stitches or solid colors, so I designed these socks to show the red, white, and blue with their best foot forward! The colors look pretty together but when knitting around a sock, they create their own pattern of swirls or stripes. To control the swirling, I added a solid and a simple slipped stitch, which adds more natural color to the design. It would be just as pretty to use navy or burgundy.

---

### SKILL LEVEL
Intermediate

### SIZE
Women's average foot, up to size 10

### FINISHED MEASUREMENTS
- Circumference: 8½ inches
- Height: 7¾ inches

### MATERIALS
- Lorna's Laces Shepherd Sock (80% superwash wool / 20% nylon, 215 yd per 2 oz skein), one skein each color
  - Liberty # 1776 [MC]
  - Natural # 0ns [CC]
- One set of four US #1 (2.25mm) double-pointed needles
- Tapestry needle

### GAUGE
28 sts and 40 rnds = 4 inches in Stockinette st

### NOTE
Keep horizontal strands loose across the front of the knitting when slipping 3 stitches.

### STITCH PATTERN

**Stranded Ribbing Stitch Pattern (multiple of 5)**
**Rounds 1–5:** *Knit 3, p2; repeat from * around.
**Rounds 6:** *Slip next 3 sts as if to purl with the yarn in front, p2; repeat from * around.

### DIRECTIONS

#### Leg
With MC, cast on 60 sts, divided evenly over 3 needles. Join, being careful not to twist, and begin Stranded Ribbing. When ribbing measures 7", work heel.

## Heel

Place 30 sts on 2 needles for instep, making certain that the
  instep begins and ends with a purl st. Place remaining
  30 sts on one needle to work heel.

**Row 1:** *Slip1, k1; repeat from *.

**Row 2:** Slip 1, purl across row.

Repeat Rows 1 and 2 until heel flap measures 2¼" (28 rows),
  ending with Row 2.

### Turn Heel

**Row 1:** K17, ssk, k1, turn.

**Row 2:** Slip 1, p5, p2tog, p1, turn.

**Row 3:** Slip 1, k6, ssk, k1, turn.

**Row 4:** Slip 1, p7, p2tog, p1, turn.

**Row 5:** Slip 1, k8, ssk, k1, turn.

**Row 6:** Slip 1, p9, p2tog, p1, turn.

Continue in this way, working 1 more st between dec until all
  30 sts have been worked, ending with a WS row—18 sts.
  Break MC.

## Instep

Join CC. Knit 9 heel sts with one needle (#1). With next
needle (#2), knit 9, pick up 19 sts along edge of heel flap.
With next needle (#3), knit 3, *p2, k3; repeat from * across
30 sts from top of foot. Pick up 19 sts along edge of heel flap
and continue across first 9 heel sts. Mark this as beginning of
round—86 sts.

## Gusset

**Round 1:** Needle #1—Knit to last 3 sts, k2tog, k1,
  Needle #2—work in pattern, Needle #3—k1, ssk,
  knit to end.

**Round 2:** Knit.

Repeat these two rounds until there are 15 sts on the first
  and third needles. Work even until sock measures 1½"
  shorter than foot length.

## Toe

Change to MC for toe, joining yarn at beginning of needle #2.
  This is the new beginning of round.

**Round 1:** Needle #1—Knit to last 3 sts, k2tog,
  Needle #2 —Knit 1, ssk, knit to last 3 sts, k2tog, k1,
  Needle# 3—Knit 1, ssk, knit to end.

**Round 2:** Knit.

Repeat these two rounds until 20 sts remain.

Graft toe sts using kitchener st. Weave in ends.

# WISDOM *on the* FLY

Waiting in another airport somewhere, on my way to somewhere. . . . I really can't remember, as I travel so often to teach and attend shows. Trip after trip, flight after flight, my knitting is always with me, even after the 9/11 security changes. Long, straight needles are what the TSA looks for, and they aren't suited for knitting on an airplane anyway. When I travel I usually knit on circular needles because they pass through security easily, they don't poke my neighbor in the seat next to me, and they don't get snapped in half when I shove my knitting back in my bag.

If you've traveled by air since 9/11, you won't be surprised to hear that on one of my trips my flight was delayed. Not a 10-minute delay, or even a delay with a time estimate, just a "delayed indefinitely" announcement with instructions to wait for further updates. Every seat at the gate had already been taken, so I sat down on the carpet, opened my travel backpack, and pulled out my knitting. I was working on a small, simple project—a child's sweater done in seed stitch on large needles—that didn't require much concentration, so I could still look around and people-watch.

Nearby was an elderly woman in a wheelchair; her husband was standing behind her. They were both watching me knit and smiling. When I smiled back, the woman told me how much she used to enjoy knitting. She had been unable to knit for a long time because her hands were stiff and knotted from arthritis. Her husband was eager to tell me about all the beautiful things she used to make. They asked about my project and watched me work the stitches: knit one, purl one, knit one, purl one. The woman recognized the seed stitch pattern and couldn't resist asking if she could work just a few stitches. I put the needles in her hands and she slowly started working across the row. Watching her take pleasure in this simple act was a tender moment. Her husband enjoyed it as much as she did.

After making a few stitches, the woman thanked me and handed back the needles. The couple continued to pass the time with me, telling me about their life together. They were both pastors of a church in Mississippi. Their business card had her information printed on one side, his on the other. One of them would start telling a story about their church or their children, and the other would finish. I didn't say much; I just listened to their combined years of wisdom and joy.

# Kid's Two-tone Zippered Hoodie

This child's sweater is similar to the one I was knitting on that trip. It's loose-fitting and the sleeves are meant to be rolled up or down so that a child can wear it for a few years. I also added a hood and zipper for extra "kid comfort." The design is knit back and forth, but please: If you take it with you on a plane, use circulars out of courtesy to your row mate!

SKILL LEVEL
Intermediate

SIZES
2 (4, 6-8, 10)

FINISHED MEASUREMENTS
- Chest: 26 (28, 31, 33) inches
- Length: 14 (15½, 18½, 21½) inches

MATERIALS
- Aurora Yarns Ornaghi Filati Tibet [55% wool/40% acrylic/5% rayon); 110 yd/100m per 100g skein],
  - two (three, three, three) skeins Green tweed #880 [A]
  - two (three, three, three) skeins Tan tweed #216 [B]
- US #8 (5mm) knitting needles
- Two separating zippers to match yarn colors 12 (13½, 16½, 19½)" long or cut at top edge to correct length
- Tapestry needle

GAUGE
14 sts and 20 rows = 4 inches in seed st

NOTES
Back is worked using intarsia method, working half of back in A and half in B. Twisting the colors at the color change will prevent holes.

Keep one stitch at each edge in Stockinette for smoother seams.

STITCH PATTERN

| KEY |
| --- |
| □ k on RS, p on WS |
| ⊡ p on RS, k on WS |

**Seed Stitch (odd number of stitches)**
**Row 1 (RS):** Knit 1, *p1, k1; repeat to end.
**Row 2 (WS):** Purl 1, *p1, k1; repeat to last 2 sts, p2.

## DIRECTIONS

### Back

With A, cast on 23 (25, 27, 29) sts, join B, and cast on another 23 (25, 27, 29) sts. Work in seed st, maintaining colors as established and keeping one st at each edge and at center join in Stockinette st. When back measures 7½ (8½, 11, 13)", place marker at side seams for underarm. Continue until back measures 14 (15½, 18½, 21½)". Bind off all sts.

### Right Front

With A, cast on 23 (25, 27, 29) sts. Working seed st until front measures 7½ (8½, 11, 13)", place marker at side seams for underarm. Continue until front measures 12 (13½, 16½, 19½)", shape neck. At neck edge (RS) bind off 5 (5, 6, 6) sts. Continuing in seed st, dec 1 st at every neck edge 4 (5, 5, 5) times, making decs 1 st in from edge. Work even until front measures same as back to shoulder. Bind off.

### Left Front

With B, cast on 23 (25, 27, 29) sts. Working seed st until front measures 7½ (8½, 11, 13)", place marker at side seams for underarm. Continue until front measures 12 (13½, 16½, 19½)", shape neck. At neck edge (WS), bind off 5 (5, 6, 6) sts. Continuing in seed stitch, dec 1 st at every neck edge 4 (5, 5, 5) times, making decs 1 st in from edge. Work even until front measures same as back to shoulder. Bind off. Sew shoulder seams.

### Right Sleeve

Between armhole markers, use B to pick up 47 (49, 53, 59) sts. Working in seed st, dec 1 st at each edge every 6th row 10 (11, 11, 12) times—27 (27, 31, 35) sts. Work even until sleeve measures 10 (11, 12, 14)", ending after a WS row. Change to A, knit 1 row. Change to seed st and work even for 3". Bind off all sts.

### Left Sleeve

Between markers, use A to pick up 47 (49, 53, 59) sts. Working in seed st, dec 1 st at each edge every 6th row 10 (11, 11, 12) times—27 (27, 31, 35) sts. Work even until sleeve measures 10 (11, 12, 14)", ending after a WS row. Change to B, knit 1 row. Change to seed st and work even for 3". Bind off all sts.

Sew side and sleeve seams, keeping cuff seams "butted together flat" so they can be turned up or rolled down as needed. Weave in ends.

## Hood

Beginning at right front neck edge, use circular needle and B to pick up approximately 10 (11,12, 12) sts to shoulder and 9 (10, 11, 11) to center back, join A and pick up matching amounts around remainder of neck edge. Keeping 2 center back sts in Stockinette st (one in each color), work in seed st and AT THE SAME TIME increase 1 st on each side of center back sts every RS row 10 times—29 (31, 33, 33) sts on each side. Work even in seed st until height of hood is 8 (8½, 9, 10)". Place half the stitches on another needle. Fold hood in half, right side together, and bind off using 3-needle bind-off method. Weave in ends.

## Three-Needle Bind-Off Join

Put right needle through 1st stitch on front needle then through 1st stitch on back needle, knit as usual. Repeat for 2nd stitch. Two stitches now are on right needle. Lift right-most stitch over last stitch knit and off the needle. One stitch now bound off. Repeat across.

## Zipper

Measure precise length of sweater front from hem to neck edge. Mark both zippers with this length. Unzip zippers. Use matching thread to make a new stopper at the top. Cut off excess zipper above stopper, leaving ½" and pulling out extra zipper teeth using pliers or tweezers. Zip two sides together and pin to sweater fronts, leaving teeth exposed. Pin in place. Using sewing thread, backstitch zippers in place, folding excess at top of zippers to inside.

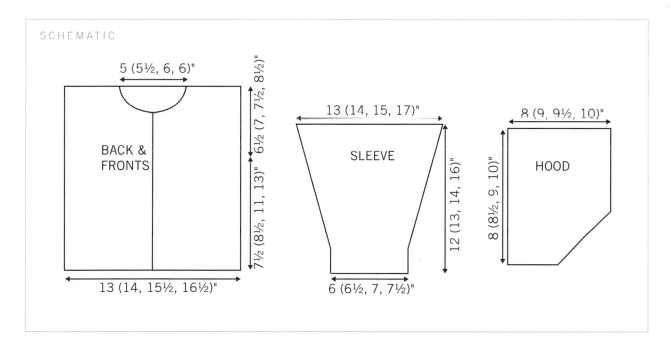

SCHEMATIC

5 (5½, 6, 6)"

6½ (7, 7½, 8½)"

BACK & FRONTS

7½ (8½, 11, 13)"

13 (14, 15½, 16½)"

13 (14, 15, 17)"

SLEEVE

12 (13, 14, 16)"

6 (6½, 7, 7½)"

8 (9, 9½, 10)"

HOOD

8 (8½, 9, 10)"

# FROM MINNESOTA
## *with* LOVE

There's a yarn shop in St. Paul, Minnesota, that's been there for as long as I can remember: 3 Kittens Yarn Shoppe. The owner's name was Karen (pronounced "CAR-en"). I knew about the store not only because I had taught a few times at a local Minnesota knitting convention, but also because I have family living nearby. Silly as it was, one of the first things about Karen that caught my attention was that she talked like my Minnesotan family members, peppering her conversation with such phrases as "Don't cha know?" and "Oh yaaah." I guess it made her feel like family right from the start.

I met Karen not at her store but at one of the knitting conventions, where she was a vendor. I loved visiting her booth, which in addition to beautiful yarns was packed with books, kits, buttons, patterns, and other items—a veritable treasure chest of knitting novelties. Between classes I would dash to her booth, where I would inevitably find something new and exciting. But I also found a friendly person who was happy to see me, and would always think to ask about my kids or my Minnesota family.

Because my relatives live just an hour south of the Twin Cities, I often combined business with pleasure, making plans to visit them while I was in town. On one trip I thought it would be fun to bring along my daughter, who at the time was just out of junior high. Our plan was to begin the trip at the convention, then drive south to stay with family. I had teaching assignments scheduled, so Grace was on her own during the day, and at 14 years old she thought all that free time was boring. On the last day of the show, after we had already checked out of our hotel room, Grace had no place to go while she waited for me to finish teaching. Karen, who by then was a trusted friend, let Grace pile up some coats and bags of yarn in a small curtained area behind her booth and take a nice little nap while the yarn world purred on around her. Sounds cozy, doesn't it?

After I had decided to sell my yarn company, Karen told me that she was also considering selling the store, which she had owned for 24 years. It was an honor to be trusted with such confidential information, and to be asked for advice.

# Three Cozy Kittens

In all our years of friendship and business together, it never occurred to me to ask Karen about the origins of the name of her shop. But since we both like cats, and she always used three cats in her logo, I created a simple toy kitten in her honor and as a tribute to all those years of owning 3 Kittens. Once you start knitting, there's no reason to stop at just three. Litters come in all sizes!

SKILL LEVEL
Easy

SIZE
One size

FINISHED MEASUREMENTS
- Width (flat): 6 inches
- Height: 10 inches

MATERIALS
- Caron Simply Soft Shadows [100% acrylic; 150 yd/137m per 85g skein], one skein per kitty, colors
  - Pearl Frost #0001
  - Dark Moss #0006
  - Opal Twist #0008
- One set of four US #7 (4.5mm) double-pointed needles
- Embroidery floss or yarns for face
- Polyester or other stuffing
- Tapestry needle

GAUGE

20 sts and 28 rnds = 4 inches in Stockinette st

## STITCH PATTERN

### Seed Stitch Pattern
**Round 1:** *Knit 1, p1; repeat from *.
**Round 2:** *Purl 1, k1; repeat from *.

## DIRECTIONS

Cast on 60 sts and divide evenly over 3 needles. Join, being careful not to twist. Place marker for beginning of round. Work in seed st until piece measures 10" from cast-on.

### Ears
Knit 10 sts, turn.
Purl same 10 sts, turn.
Ssk, k6, k2tog, turn.
Purl across, turn.
Ssk, k4, k2tog, turn.
Purl across, turn.
Ssk, k2, k2tog, turn.
Purl across, turn.
Ssk, k2tog, turn.
P2tog, end off.

### Top of Head
Join yarn to next st. Bind off 10 sts. Work next ear. Join yarn to next st and work another ear immediately. Bind off 10 sts. Work last ear.

### Base
Cast on 24 sts. Work in seed st for 1". Bind off.

### Tail
Cast on 12 sts and divide evenly over 3 needles. Join, being careful not to twist. Knit every round for 2". *Knit 2, k2tog; repeat from * around—9 sts. Knit every round for 2". *Knit 1, k2tog; repeat from * around—6 sts. Move all sts to one needle and continue using "I-cord" method: *Knit across all sts. Push stitches to right end of double-pointed needle. Repeat from * until tail measures 6" or desired length. Cut yarn and using tapestry needle, thread end through remaining sts. Pull tight and fasten off yarn. Weave in ends.

### Finishing
Sew top of head and around ears. Add embroidered face. Stuff lightly. Sew base to cast on edge. Tie ribbon tightly around neck. Sew tail to body.

# CIRCLE *of* LIFE,
# CIRCLE *of* FRIENDSHIP

As much as I would like to avoid life's sad times, I know that they're inevitable. In God's goodness and love, He's sometimes given me new friends during painful experiences.

Laura and I didn't meet through my knitting. We met through one of my dearest friends in the world. My friend was dying, and Laura was her hospice nurse. I couldn't be with my friend very often during the last days of her illness, so I took comfort in getting to know Laura—her loving generosity and willingness to care for my friend impressed me—and in knowing that Laura was there for her. She was literally a joy to be around: She brought laughter and fun to a place of illness and pain and fear.

Over the days that I visited my friend, Laura and I found that we had many things in common: our families, our faith, even our husbands' names. When the time came that my friend slipped away, Laura and I had built our own friendship, tied together with love, sadness, hope, and knitting. Laura shares her gifts—the care and comfort she gives to her dying patients, and her knitting—with so many lives: her family, friends, and community. She is especially generous with her patients, reading to them, knitting gifts for them, teaching them to knit, sharing yarn, knitting needles, and patterns.

# Memory Lap Throw

This lap throw is symbolic of the comfort that Laura passes on to so many people: So many lives touched, and a throw with so many yarns mixed together and blended to cozy beauty. One of the projects that our terminally ill friend was working on right before her death was a small blanket that used a wide variety of yarn and colors. When Laura and I were sorting through her yarn and projects, Laura decided to take the half-finished blanket and complete it. The blanket I've designed is similar in that it uses many yarns that vary not just in weight but in texture. This allows you to choose yarns as you work, making the project completely random and spontaneous to knit.

SKILL LEVEL
Easy

SIZE
One size

FINISHED MEASUREMENTS
40 inches square (plus fringe)

MATERIALS
- Universal Yarns Panda [100% bamboo; 98 yd/90m per 50g skein], one skein #10
- Universal Yarns Ever [68% polyamide, 15% acrylic, 14% wool, 3% glitter; 109 yd/100m per 50g skein], one skein #10
- Universal Yarns Curly Mohair [72% mohair, 16% wool, 12% polyamide; 131 yd/120m per 50g skein], two skeins #41
- Universal Yarns Precious [96% polyamide, 3% polyester, 1% glitter; 82 yd/75m per 50g skein], four skeins #15
- Universal Yarns Vanessa [50% viscose, 50% dralon; 109 yd/100m per 50g skein], two skeins #1509
- Universal Yarns Jewel [57% acrylic, 28% mohair, 9% cotton, 6% polyester; 82 yd/75m per 50g skein], three skeins #02
- Universal Yarns Moods [50% wool, 50% acrylic; 197 yd/180m per 100g skein], one skein #1511
- Universal Yarns Classic Worsted [80% acrylic, 20% wool; 197 yd/180m per 100g skein], three skeins #650BLK
- Universal Yarns Bellagio [40% polyamide, 60% cotton; 109 yd/100m per 50g skein], one skein #36
- Universal Yarns Aster Magic [26% viscose, 18% dralon, 56% polyamide; 98 yd/90m per 50g skein], three skeins #LDG9150
- Universal Yarns Tango [50% superwash merino wool, 50% fine dralon; 22 yd/20m per 50g skein], one skein #588
- Universal Yarns Elite [93% acrylic, 7% glitter yarn; 71 yd/65m per 50g skein], two skeins #12
- Universal Yarns Pace [75% super wash wool, 25% polyamide; 220 yd/200m per 50g skein], one skein #01

- Universal Yarns Deluxe Worsted Tweed [100% wool, 220 yd/200m per 100g skein], two skeins #08
- Universal Yarns Rebecca [38% polyamide, 37% acrylic, 25% mohair, 71 yd/65m per 50g skein], one skein #16
- Wisdom Yarns Bamboo Splash [100% bamboo; 87 yd/80m per 50g skein], four skeins #105
- Wisdom Yarns Poems [100% wool; 109 yd/100m per 50g skein], two skeins #571
- Fibranatura Senstional [100% superwash merino wool; 90 yd/83m per 50g skein], one skein #40801
- Fibranatura Birch [50% superwash merino wool, 30% alpaca, 20% silk; 120 yd/110m per 50g skein], one skein #40307
- Fibranatura Oak [60% superwash merino wool, 20% linen, 205 silk; 175 yd/160m per 50g skein], two skeins #40257
- Fibranatura Links [100% organic cotton; 87 yd/80m per 50g skein], one skein #41201
- Fibranatura Trellis [50% wool, 14% baby alpaca, 29% silk, 10% fine mohair; 88 yd/80m per 50g skein], two skeins #40029
- One 32-inch US #13 (9mm) circular needle

## GAUGE
8 sts and 14 rows = 4 inches in garter st

## PATTERN
Randomly use any two yarns held together and knit one row.

## NOTES
Entire throw is knit in garter stitch (knit every row), holding two strands together and changing yarns every row. The ends are left long at the beginning and end of each row then tied to make self-fringe. TANGO and PRECIOUS, bulky yarns, are used single-stranded.

## DIRECTIONS

With any combination of 2 strands, cast on 100 sts, leaving an 8" tail. Knit one row. Cut yarns, leaving an 8" tail at the end of the row. Tie next 2-strand combination of yarns to ends from previous row close to the knitting using an overhand knot. Knit one row. Repeat this single row until throw measures 40" or desired width. Bind off all sts.

### Finishing
Drape throw over the edge of a table or shower rod. Comb fringe to smooth and straighten it. Trim fringe even. Repeat for other end.

# RANDOM ACTS
## *of* BIRTHDAY HAPPINESS

One of the most enjoyable things about knitting in public is that it gives people an open invitation to talk to me by showing an interest in what I'm doing. My daughter and I like to joke that we've never met a stranger; everyone is just a friend we don't know yet. It's an aspect of traveling that gives us something to look forward to, because we always know we're going to enjoy meeting someone new even before the trip has begun.

On the way back home from my trip to Scotland, I stopped over in Washington, D.C. for a couple of days. While I was there I bought a skein of beautiful purple ribbon yarn. It called out to me at the yarn shop, practically begging to be knitted: "Touch me! Buy me! Take me home!" (If you love yarn as much as I do I expect you may have heard a skein or two speak to you—though you probably wouldn't want to admit that to someone who doesn't knit.) When I was packing, that skein of amethyst ribbon refused to go into the suitcase I was planning to check, insisting that it belonged in my carry-on. Its intentions were obvious: This skein wanted to have its way with me on the six-hour plane ride home. (Even its name—Tartlette—sounds like a tease.) Eventually I gave in. (What can I say? I'm a pushover when it comes to gorgeous yarn.)

As soon as I had settled into my seat on the plane, I released Tartlette from my carry-on bag, pulled out the only needles I had with me, and cast on a few stitches. I didn't have enough yarn to make a large project, I didn't have any stitch dictionaries with me to plan an intricate stitch pattern, and I was too tired to design something complicated.

As one of the flight attendants walked down the aisle, she noticed that I was knitting. She was beautiful, with dark skin and a contagious smile, and her uniform was the same shade of purple as my wonderful ribbon. She immediately began teasing me that she wanted a birthday present, though I guessed she was only joking when she said it was her birthday.

I sometimes like to give myself little challenges. Silly things, like giving myself fifteen minutes to clean a room, or keeping a pace of thirteen miles per hour on my bicycle. The flight attendant's playful joke became one of those opportunities to challenge myself and have fun while enjoying my new ribbon—and possibly make someone's day. Until that point I was really only experimenting with a swatch without knowing what I would make with the yarn. But once the flight attendant connected with me, I knew: I would try to knit a scarf so I could give it to her at the end of the flight. She didn't know what I had planned, of course, but every time she passed by on her walk through the cabin, she checked on my work. Her sense of humor entertained me and all of the passengers within earshot, making the trip go by quickly.

By the time we arrived in Sacramento, I had finished my project. The pilots and flight attendants were all standing at the cabin door as I left the plane. I thanked them, draped the scarf over my flight attendant's neck, and wished her a happy birthday. With all the other passengers behind me waiting to exit, there was no time to stop and explain myself, or even to be thanked. It was simply my way of thanking her for sharing the gift of her humor—and for inspiring me to share my gift, too.

# Happy Birthday Ribbon Scarf

I could see after just a few rows of working with the ribbon that the needles I had on hand were far too small for it. My solution was to work extra wraps around the needle and drop them on the following row, creating elongated stitches that really enhance the ribbon's beautiful drape. This scarf is clearly more a fashion accessory than for warmth. The good news is that it only takes one skein and a couple of hours, so you can make many of them!

SKILL LEVEL
Beginner

SIZE
One size

FINISHED MEASUREMENTS
• Width: approximately 4 inches
• Length: approximately 36 inches

MATERIALS
• Knit One Crochet Too Tartlette [50% cotton / 50% nylon; 75 yd/69m per 50g skein], one skein color #13
• US #9 (5.5mm) knitting needles

GAUGE
14 sts and 16 rows = 4 inches in pattern st

STITCH PATTERN

**Elongated Garter Stitch**
**Rows 1-2:** Knit.
**Row 3:** Knit across, wrapping yarn around needle twice for each stitch.
**Row 4:** Knit across, dropping extra wraps.

DIRECTIONS

Cast on 16 sts. Work in Elongated Garter Stitch until about 1 yard of yarn remains. Bind off. Weave in ends.

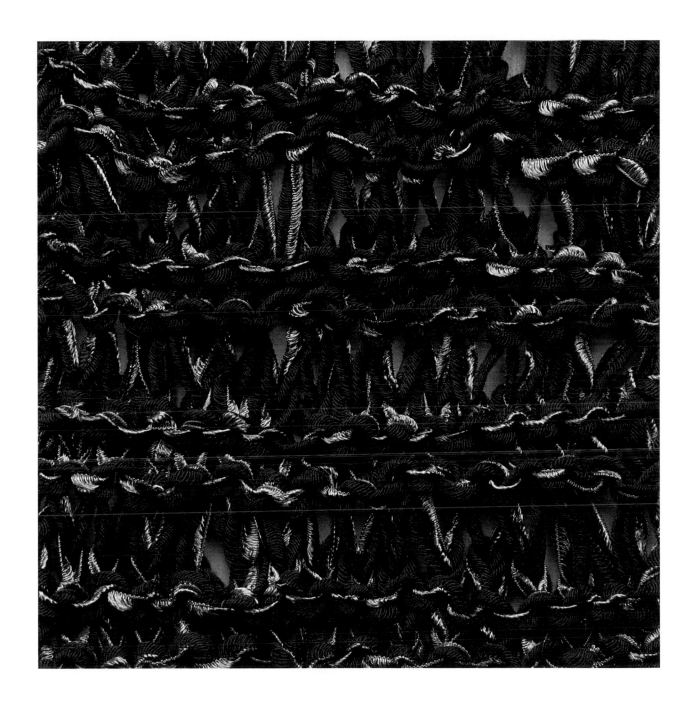

# *a* NEW
# GIRL SCOUT LAW

Some of my friends asked if I would help teach their Girl Scout troop—a group of ten 10-year-olds—how to knit. I'm used to teaching adults, mostly women, who already know how to knit, and I mainly teach advanced design or technique classes so that my students can use their skills in new ways. But little girls who've never touched yarn or needles? I knew I'd be in for a challenging afternoon—or, at the very least, an entertaining one.

My friends and I planned what we thought would be a fun lesson that included making knitting needles. We purchased wooden dowels for the needles and polymer clay for the endcaps. The girls had a blast working with the clay. First they softened the clay and mixed special colors, then made endcaps out of kitty faces or flowers, or decorated round shapes with bright polka dots. While the clay was baking, the girls sanded and polished the rough dowels with such energy and diligence, they made the smoothest wooden knitting needles I'd ever touched. Once their caps had cooled down, they glued them to ends of the sanded dowels and were ready to learn to knit.

Well, that was the idea, anyway. The girls were so pleased and excited about the beautiful needles they had made that they forgot they still needed to learn to knit. Suddenly ten 10-year-old girls were running around, waving knitting needles. My friends and I all started shouting at them to stop. Thankfully no one was hurt, but I had to laugh: In all the classes I've taught, at all the conventions and trade shows I've attended, knitting needle injuries have never really been an issue.

Eventually the girls calmed down enough to learn how to knit two squares, which they then stitched together to make a little beanbag. (Some girls used theirs as doll pillows.) Those Girl Scouts learned another valuable lesson, too: DON'T RUN WITH KNITTING NEEDLES!

# Scout's Honor Beanbag
## and Homemade Knitting Needles

The squares that my Girl Scout students knitted for their beanbags weren't felted. I didn't know what yarns they'd be bringing along, so I had them line their knitted bags with a little pouch made from discarded pantyhose so that the filling wouldn't leak out through the knitted stitches. For this project, though, I chose a wool-blend yarn that would felt, not only because felting eliminates uneven stitching and mistakes (which beginners find discouraging) but also because you can fill the beanbags with beads or beans or popcorn without worrying about lining them. I also like that this yarn is variegated (it changes colors), which inspires young girls (or any new knitters) to keep knitting till they get to the next color, and then the next, and so on.

---

## Beanbag

SKILL LEVEL
Beginner

SIZES
One size

FINISHED MEASUREMENTS
Square after Felting: approximately 4 inches

MATERIALS
- Patons SWS [70% wool, 30% soy; 110 yd/100m per 80g skein], one skein each
  - color # 70418
  - color #70310
  - color #70580
- US #10½ (6.5mm) knitting needles, store-bought or homemade
- Sewing thread and needle
- Poly-fil™ beads or popcorn
- Tapestry needle

GAUGE

12 sts and 16 rows = 4 inches in Stockinette st (before felting)

STITCH PATTERN

**Stockinette Stitch**

**Row 1 (RS):** Knit one row.

**Row 2:** Purl one row.

Repeat Rows 1 and 2.

NOTE

Gauge is not important as the finished piece will be felted (shrunk). It is the perfect beginner project, as the felting will hide errors.

DIRECTIONS

Cast on 20 sts. Work in Stockinette st for 50 rows. Bind off.

Fold rectangle in half to make a square. Sew both side edges and halfway across the end, leaving a 2" opening.

Place in washing machine with other squares or some towels. Run regular wash cycle using hot water and detergent. When completely felted, stretch and tug square into shape and allow it to dry. Fill with poly-fil beads or popcorn. Sew remaining opening with sewing thread. Trim excess fuzz if desired.

# Homemade Knitting Needles

Beginner

## MATERIALS

- Variety of Polymer clay in various colors (I like Sculpey Clay)
- Toaster oven or oven
- Cooking sheet with foil
- ¼" dowel cut into 10" lengths
- Pencil sharpener
- 200 grit sand paper
- Fine steel wool
- Wax paper
- Hot glue gun and glue

## DIRECTIONS

Make fun, colored balls of clay about the size of a small marble. Add faces, initials, textures, or more color swirls. Gently push the dowel about halfway into the ball of clay. Remove the dowel and place the clay onto a foil-lined cooking sheet. Bake for 10—15 minutes at 200 degrees. It is fine to bake longer but not hotter. The clay should be hard when it is finished.

While the clay is baking, sharpen one end of the dowel using a pencil sharpener. Use the sand paper to smooth the tip and flatten it a little bit. Sand the entire dowel until it is very smooth with no snags anywhere. Repeat the process with the steel wool, then with the wax paper. When the clay ends have cooled, use hot glue to secure them to the flat end of the dowels.

# UNDER DEEP COVER

Knitting took over my professional life after I started Lorna's Laces. In addition to running the company, I was often invited to teach at yarn shops and knitting conventions around the country. As the business grew, I worked very hard and hired help, but I had to delegate many of the things I enjoyed doing. Eventually I wasn't able to do my favorite thing—knitting—anymore. After finally deciding to sell the company, I immediately began planning the trip of my dreams: to Scotland.

While growing up, I had a best friend whose mother was Scottish and whose father was British. Her parents had beautiful accents and traditions and a strong sense of a heritage, all of which were very exotic to me. Even as far back as the sixth grade, when I was assigned to write a report on Scotland, the more I learned about it, the more I wanted to see it. Years later I read some historical novels that piqued my curiosity even more.

It was going to be a long trip—a few days in London, three weeks in Scotland, and a few days in Washington, D.C., on the way back to California—more than a month in all. I had studied a little Scottish history and wanted to travel around the Highlands, to visit out-of-the-way places where tourists wouldn't normally go. Naturally, one of the most important things on my to-do list was to plan a knitting project to bring with me. For this trip, the project needed to be portable, last thirty days, be simple enough so I could still sightsee, and yield a memento I could treasure for years.

Suddenly, it came to me: If each day I knit a mitered square, starting at a corner and increasing until it measured twelve inches from corner to corner diagonally, I wouldn't have to limit my yarn choices or do a gauge swatch—I could just cast on and make a square. With that realization, my plan evolved an advantageous perk: Buy a little bit of yarn every day in each town I passed through.

Knitting a small square each day turned out to be fun and easy to manage. I would sit in pubs, knitting and listening to local musicians, and inevitably a woman would comment that she wished she had thought to "bring her workin'," then tell me about an out-of-the-way yarn shop in a nearby town where I could find the yarn for my next square. I kept a small notebook documenting my travels and where I had purchased my yarn, then that night, before going to sleep, I sewed the newly knitted square to my burgeoning blanket. I realize that I could have knit the blanket in such a way as to avoid sewing it, but then I would have had to haul the entire blanket-in-process everywhere, thereby defeating the purpose of my convenient "square-a-day" plan.

Of course, there were other things about the trip besides knitting that I enjoyed. In addition to the dozens of yarn shops I visited, I went to a famous spinning mill. I also loved that there were so many other Lornas. At one yarn shop I was given a tour of their sweater production area and was jokingly told that they'd be happy to hire me as they were "short one Lorna," being down to four Lornas from their usual five. With my fair skin and deep red hair, I could have easily been mistaken for a native Scotswoman—if only I could find a way to let people know my name without speaking!

## Square-a-Day Blanket

This blanket was designed specifically with the idea of a knitter's vacation in mind. Knitters are always looking for an excuse to stop at every yarn shop we pass by, and by using this approach, you can buy one skein in every store, every day of your trip, knit it immediately (without even swatching for gauge!), and return home with a blanket-sized journal of your trip.

Easy

Full size blanket

FINISHED MEASUREMENTS
- Width: 60 inches
- Length: 72 inches

MATERIALS
- Patons Divine [76.5% acrylic, 10.5% wool, 10.5% mohair, 2.5% polyester; 142 yd/129m per 100g skein],
  - two skeins color # 06011
  - one skein color #06230
- Patons SWS [70% wool, 30% soy; 110 yd/100m per 80g skein], three skeins each
  - color # 70310
  - color # 70013
- Patons Brilliant [69% acrylic, 19% nylon, 12% polyester; 166 yd/151m per 50g skein], three skeins each
  - color # 03320
  - color # 3314
- Patons Decor [75% acrylic, 25% wool; 210 yd/192m per 100g skein],
  - two skeins color # 01625
  - one skein each
    - color # 01631
    - color # 01627
    - color # 01633

- color # 01698
- color # 01614
- Patons Shetland Chunky Tweeds [72% acrylic, 25 % wool, 3% viscose; 123 yd/113m per 85g skein], two skeins color # 67031
- Patons Bohemian [81% polyester, 19% acrylic; 68 yd/62m per 80g skein],
  - two skeins color # 11310
  - one skein each
    - color # 11013
    - color # 11430
- US #9 (5.5mm) knitting needles
- One large stitch marker
- Tapestry needle

GAUGE
Will vary from 3 sts = 1" to 4 sts = 1" in garter st

NOTES
Work this blanket one square at a time, while on a trip. It's fun to buy just a skein of yarn here and there as souvenirs of different locations, then knit just one square each day and sew them together each evening back in your hotel room. By the time you get home, you'll have a whole blanket (or good start on one!) and memories locked up in a beautiful memory blanket to treasure and remember your trip.

COLORS
Divide the yarn into light, medium, and dark colors. Use one of each group for each square, starting at the corner and working increases until the sides measure 12". For the lighter weight yarns, use two strands.

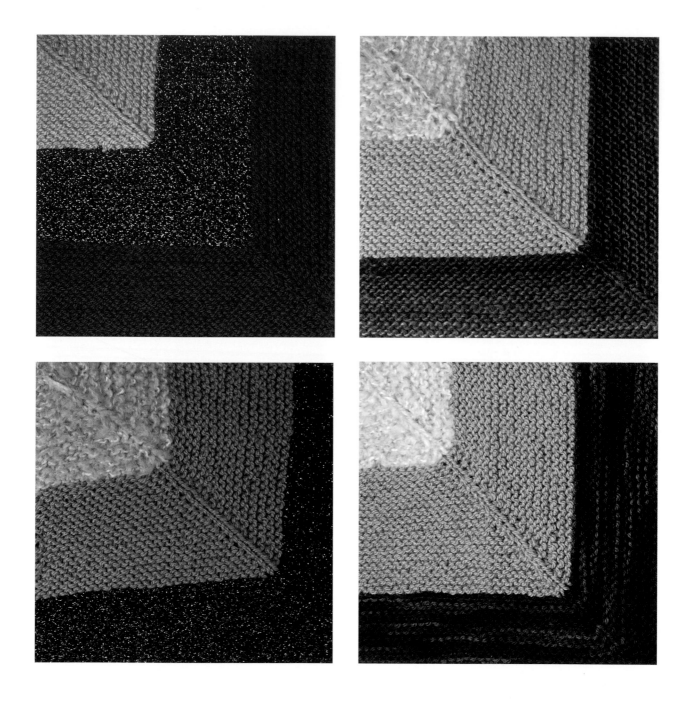

## DIRECTIONS

With light color, cast on 3 sts. Place a marker on each side of the middle stitch. WS rows: Knit to marker, purl 1, knit to end. RS rows: Knit to marker, make 1 by making a twisted loop onto the right needle, slip marker, knit 1, slip marker, make 1 by making a loop that twists the opposite direction of the previous one (mirror image), knit to end. Work these 2 rows until one edge measures about 4". Change to medium color and continue pattern until one edge measures about 8". Change to dark color and continue pattern until square measures 12". Bind off. Weave in one end of each color, leave the remaining end of yarn for sewing the squares together.

*Note:* Each square may have a different number of stitches when it is bound off. The number of sts is not important and the gauge is not important. Only the size of the finished square is important.

Make 30 squares. Sew the squares together 5 across and 6 down. Weave in ends.

# a CHILD'S
# SIMPLE REQUEST

For more than twenty years I lived in the foothills of the Sierra Nevada, not far from South Lake Tahoe. On my two-acre property I raised sheep, angora rabbits, chickens, ducks, and llamas, along with the customary dogs and cats. My house was on a busy corner, so friends and neighbors would always notice if there were a new lamb in the pasture or one of the sheep had escaped. Sometimes strangers would pull over to take pictures of the llamas or feed them apples from my apple tree.

One day my friend Martha called and asked if she could bring her eight-year-old daughter Mary and a couple of Mary's friends to visit the animals and to see my overstuffed yarn room, which grew partly out of my yarn production business, and partly out of my love for knitting. Martha's husband and mine worked together at the fire department, and since our families had spent some time together I had encouraged Martha to visit me.

When they arrived for their tour, the three girls chased the chickens and ducks around the yard and petted the cats and dogs. Then we picked apples and went out to the pasture. I had two llamas and two sheep—though it would be more accurate to say that I had two llamas, each of whom had a pet sheep. (Llamas are very alert and protective, and really seem to like having someone to take care of. On one occasion they proved their mettle by putting up a good fight with a mountain lion!) The girls fed them apples—miraculously, no one got spit on—then we proceeded to the yarn room.

No one really knows what to say when they see my yarn room. It's a little overwhelming, unless you own a yarn shop. There are walls and walls of yarn and books and sweaters. There are also other crafts in abundance: rubber stamps, scrapbooking papers, paints, and woodcrafts. (As I said, it's a bit overwhelming.) The girls were dazzled by the amount of yarn that one woman could own. I let them rummage through some of the large yarn bins and told them to choose colors they might like to knit with. They had all learned to knit in the private school they attended, and knew enough about it to be able to knit a simple first garment. Of all three girls, though, only Mary made a creative connection with the yarn and its beautiful colors, combining red and purple and green with pink and baby blue and orange. Mary's rainbow of fun, wild, bright yarn inspired her to knit a garment of her own design: a poncho, for herself.

Mary and I talked a little bit about how to make the poncho, and I wrote down some notes about the number of stitches to cast on, how to increase, and how to change colors. The next day her mother e-mailed a photo of the half-finished poncho, which Mary completed just a few days later. It was a carnival of colors, perfect for a little girl to express her creativity.

I was impressed, of course, and Mary was proud. She was such a naturally gifted knitter that she only needed a nudge in the right direction. She wasn't afraid to try because no one told her that it would be hard to knit without a pattern, or scary to knit something until it was the right size.

I hope that Mary continues to find ways to use her God-given gift, which is much more than her capacity for knitting, or combining colors, or learning quickly. She has a confidence and fearlessness that I'm sure must serve her well in other aspects of her life. I'm honored and humbled that I played a small part in igniting her creative spark.

# A Fearless Girl's Poncho

The poncho "pattern" I gave Mary was more like a recipe. It told her when and where to make increases and encouraged her to change colors as she wished. Her poncho colors were quite random and free. This poncho is the same design but the yarns and colors have been spelled out for you. As we get older, many of us grow inhibited when playing with colors or we find ourselves making even stripes instead of letting the stripes flow randomly. Allow your inner child to come out when changing colors on this poncho.

## SKILL LEVEL
Easy

## SIZE
Loose-fitting; sizes: toddler (teen)

## FINISHED MEASUREMENTS
Length (neck to hem): approximately 9 inches (15 inches), easily adjustable

## MATERIALS
- Lion Brand Homespun [98% acrylic/2% polyester; 185 yd/169m per 170g skein], one skein Waterfall #329 [A]
- Lion Brand Lion Suede [100% polyester; 111 yd/101m per 78g skein], one skein each
  - Seacrest Print #206 [B]
  - Teal #178 [F]
- Lion Brand Cotton Ease [50% acrylic/50% cotton; 207 yd/188m per 100g skein], one skein Lake #110 [C]
- Lion Brand Chenille Thick & Quick [91% acrylic/9% rayon; 100 yd/91m per skein*], one skein Antique White #098 [D]
- Lion Brand Jiffy [100% acrylic; 135 yd/123m per 85g skein], one skein each
  - Slate #151 [E]
  - Baby Blue #106 [H]
- Lion Brand Lion Boucle [17% acrylic/20% mohair/1% nylon; 57 yd/52m per 70g skein], one skein Wild Berries #210 [G]

- One 16-inch US #10½ (6.5mm) circular needle
- One 29-inch US #10½ (6.5mm) circular needle
- Stitch markers
- Tapestry needle

## GAUGE
12 sts and 16 rnds = 4 inches in Stockinette st with E

## NOTE
Poncho begins at the neck edge and is worked in the round downward to the hem. Increases are worked at the front and back for the full length of the poncho and at the shoulders until it is wide enough to fit over the wearer's shoulders.

## STITCH PATTERN AND COLOR SEQUENCE

With A, knit 4 rounds.
With B, knit 1 round, purl 1 round.
With C, knit 4 rounds.
With D, knit 2 rounds.
With E, knit 6 rounds.
With F, knit 1 round, purl 1 round.
With G, knit 2 rounds.
With H, knit 2 rounds.
Repeat as needed.

---

\* Because of the nature of Lion Brand Chenille Thick & Quick yarn, the company gives only the length, not the weight, of the yarn as the number of ounces can vary due to the texture of the skein.

## DIRECTIONS

With A and shorter needle, cast on 52 (60) sts loosely. Place markers to indicate the beginning of the round, then after 13th (15th) 26th ( 30th) and 39th (45th) sts. Join, being careful not to twist. Purl 1 round, knit 1 round, purl 1 round. Next round: Knit into front and back of first st, * knit to 1 st before marker, knit into front and back of next st, slip marker, knit into front and back of next st; repeat from * two more times, then knit to front and back of last st.

Continue working increases every other round while working yarn and color sequence. Cut yarn after each use and weave in ends.

When there are 19 (25) sts between markers, remove 2nd and 4th markers for shoulders and work increases only at the center front and back for the remainder of the poncho.

Repeat yarn and color sequence until poncho measures approx 9" (15)" or to desired length. Change to A. *Knit 1 round, purl 1 round; repeat from * once. Bind off. Block poncho.

SCHEMATIC

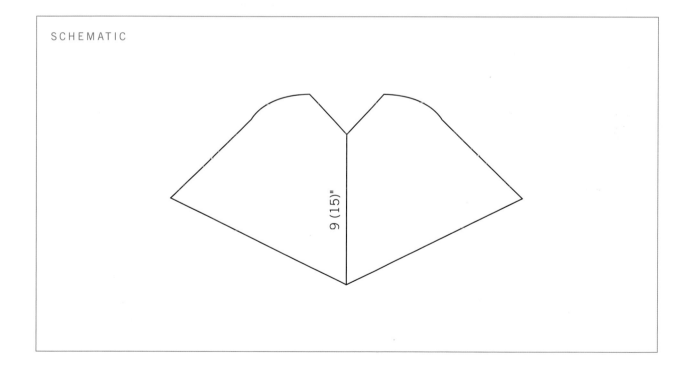

9 (15)"

# APPOINTMENT *from* HEAVEN

love teaching knitting classes. Usually my teaching assignments are at knitting conventions or retreats sponsored by yarn shop owners. I began teaching about 20 years ago when I owned Lorna's Laces and do it even more now that I'm a full-time designer.

Over the years I've come to realize that there are usually two reasons for my teaching trips. The "business" reason is pretty straightforward: to teach a class or two about a knitting technique, and to share my knitting experience with other talented knitters across the country. But every trip has a personal reason, too, and it's always an unexpected surprise. There's always at least one student—sometimes several—who touches my heart in a special way, and I've come to anticipate each trip with the question, "Who will it be?"

During a trip to Wisconsin, I met a young woman named Amy while I was between classes. We began to talk as we worked on our knitting projects, and our spiritual and creative connection was immediate as I recognized in her some of my own heart's passions. Her devotion to God is so strong that she literally radiates His love, and she's also passionate about her family and her knitting. Actually, she reminded me of my younger self, when I was just starting my yarn business, and I felt that she had the potential to achieve great things, too. I could hear the enthusiasm in her voice as she described some of her knitting projects, which sounded creative and reflected her advanced knitting skills.

Amy and I have had many occasions to talk since our first weekend together. I truly feel that God connected us, bringing her to my class to encourage me, and bringing me to Wisconsin to meet her. I need a boost of enthusiasm occasionally, something that energizes me to be creative and fresh. Amy's creativity inspires me, and I hope that I have encouraged her to pursue designing and teaching because I know that she has potential.

I'm thankful that God has given me gifts—creativity, desire, and skill—and that He wants me to use them. Each of us has something that we do well, or that we do a bit more effortlessly than others can. This is our gift, and not to use it would be an insult to the Giver. So many times I hear people put down their own talents, saying self-deprecating things because they don't want to sound proud or boastful. But there's a big difference between boastful pride and confidence. If you're talented at something, don't hide it—do it and enjoy it. You'll spread more joy that way.

# Men's Heavenly Cable Sweater

The day I met Amy, she was knitting a man's wool sweater, a very large, involved project that she was making for her husband. I can't recall all its details, but I do remember that it featured cables. As a tribute to Amy and to that day, I've designed a man's sweater that features cables and textures and is worked entirely seamlessly. Of course, there's no reason a woman couldn't wear it too!

## SKILL LEVEL
Experienced

## SIZES
Men's small (medium, large, extra-large)

## FINISHED MEASUREMENTS
- Chest: 48 (52, 56, 60) inches
- Length: 25 (27, 29, 31) inches

## MATERIALS
- Brown Sheep Nature Spun Worsted [100% wool; 245 yd/224m per 100g skein], seven (eight, nine, eleven) skeins #701 Stone
- One US #7 (4.5mm) 29-inch circular needle
- One US #7 (4.5 mm) 16-inch circular needle
- One set of four or five US #7 (4.5 mm) double-pointed needles
- Cable needle
- Stitch markers
- Tapestry needle

## GAUGE
- 22 sts and 26 rows = 4 inches in Center Cable Pattern
- 18 sts and 28 rows = 4 inches in seed st

## NOTES
Sweater is knit in the round without seams. Body is knit up to the underarms, sleeves are knit up to the underarms, then all are joined and the yoke is knit in the round with decreases forming the raglan lines. One stitch marker should be a unique color to indicate beginning of the round.

## FOLLOWING THE CHARTS
When knitting in the round, every row of the chart is read from right to left, the same way the stitches on the needles move from right to left. When making a gauge swatch, practice the 29-st Center Panel Cable, working it flat (back and forth). To do this, read all WS rows on the chart from left to right.

## Double Cable

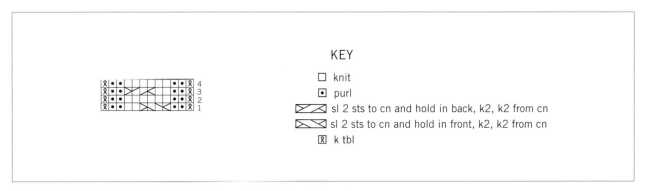

KEY

☐ knit

⊡ purl

▭ sl 2 sts to cn and hold in back, k2, k2 from cn

▭ sl 2 sts to cn and hold in front, k2, k2 from cn

⊠ k tbl

## Center Panel Cable

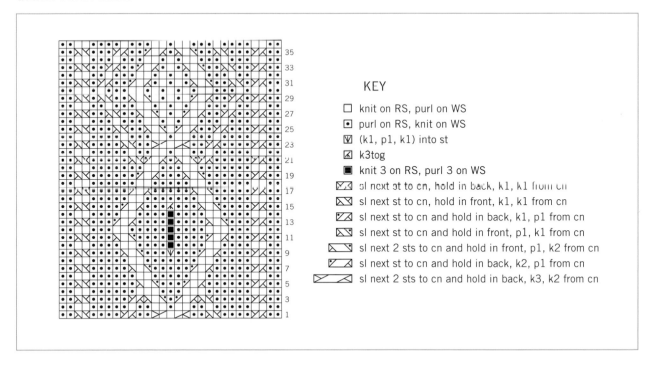

KEY

☐ knit on RS, purl on WS

⊡ purl on RS, knit on WS

Ⓥ (k1, p1, k1) into st

⊠ k3tog

■ knit 3 on RS, purl 3 on WS

▭ sl next st to cn, hold in back, k1, k1 from cn

▭ sl next st to cn, hold in front, k1, k1 from cn

▭ sl next st to cn and hold in back, k1, p1 from cn

▭ sl next st to cn and hold in front, p1, k1 from cn

▭ sl next 2 sts to cn and hold in front, p1, k2 from cn

▭ sl next st to cn and hold in back, k2, p1 from cn

▭ sl next 2 sts to cn and hold in back, k3, k2 from cn

Set up cable pattern: *Knit 7 (7, 8, 8) sts, work seed st over next 30 (36, 40, 46) sts, p2, work Double Cable over next 12 sts, work Center Panel over next 29 sts, work Double Cable over next 12 sts, p2, work seed st over next 30 (36, 40, 46) sts, knit 7 (7, 8, 8) sts, slip marker for side, repeat from * around. Continue in established patterns until body measures 15 (16, 17, 18)" from beg, ending after an odd-numbered (cable-crossing) round.

**Next rnd:** Work in pattern, slipping 7 sts before and after each marker onto holder for underarm. Do not cut yarn. Leaving sts on needle, set aside body.

## Sleeves

With double-pointed needles, cast on 58 (60, 64, 66) sts. Divide sts evenly on needles and join, being careful not to twist. Place marker for beginning of round. Work in knit 1, purl 1 ribbing for 3". Work 1 more round of ribbing, increasing 13 (13, 15, 15) sts evenly around—71 (73, 79, 81) sts. Set up cable pattern: *Knit 2 sts, work in seed st over next 5 (6, 9, 10) sts, p2, work Double Cable over next 12 sts, work Center Cable Panel over next 29 sts, work Double Cable over next 12 sts, p2, work seed st over next 5 (6, 9, 10) sts, knit 2 sts. Continue in pattern, increasing 1 st on each side of marker every 8th (8th, 8th, 6th) round 11 (14, 14, 21) times—93 (101, 107, 123) sts. Work even until sleeve measures 18 (19, 20, 21)", or desired length to underarm, ending after an odd-numbered (cable-crossing) round. Next rnd: Work in established patterns, slipping 7 sts before and after marker onto holder for underarm.

DIRECTIONS

## Body

With longer circular needle, cast on 262 (286, 306, 330) sts. Join, being careful not to twist  Place marker for beginning of round, knit 131 (143, 153, 165) sts, place marker, knit to end of round. Work in knit 1, purl 1 ribbing for 5 rounds.

## Join for Yoke

*Note:* The body and sleeves may be continuing on a different pattern round. Continue each section in pattern as needed. With yarn attached to body, work in pattern across 117 (129, 139, 151) back sts, place marker, work in pattern across 79 (87, 93, 109) left sleeve sts, place marker, work in pattern across 117 (129, 139, 151) front sts, place marker, work in pattern across 79 (87, 93, 109) right sleeve sts, place a uniquely colored marker to indicate end of round—392 (432, 464, 520) total sts.

**Round 1:** *K1, ssk, work in established pattern to 3 sts before marker, k2tog, k1; repeat from * around.

**Round 2:** *Knit 2, work in established pattern to 2 sts before marker, k2; repeat from * around.

Repeat these two rounds 32 (36, 38, 43) more times, ending after Round 1–128 (136, 152, 168) sts remain.

## Neck Edging

Removing markers, knit one round, decreasing 20 (20, 24, 34) sts evenly around—108 (116, 128, 134) sts. Work knit 1, purl 1 ribbing for 1". Bind off.

## Finishing

Graft underarm stitches using kitchener stitch. Weave in ends. Block sweater.

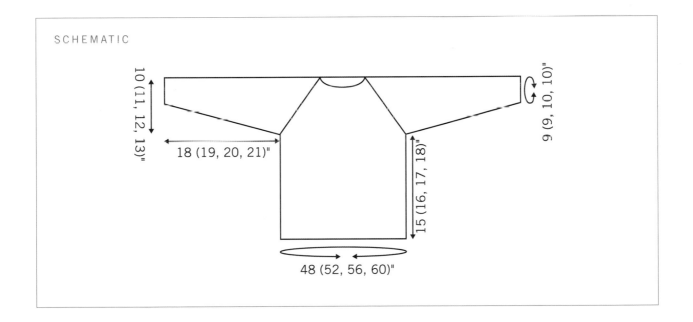

SCHEMATIC

10 (11, 12, 13)"

18 (19, 20, 21)"

9 (9, 10, 10)"

15 (16, 17, 18)"

48 (52, 56, 60)"

# JUST ENOUGH HELP

A couple of years ago I decided to go to a new knitting group in Folsom I'd heard about. After many years of working long hours to produce yarn, I finally had time to knit, and to meet other knitters. The group consisted of about a dozen women in an unstructured setting, where anyone who could knit was welcome to sit and socialize. I didn't know anyone there, and they didn't know who I was either. I introduced myself but didn't mention my yarn company. Some of the women wouldn't have heard of it, while others would have felt intimidated. So I tried my best to just blend in.

There was one woman, Sheila, who appeared to be closer in age to me than the other members, who were mostly older and retired. She was sitting alone but seemed anxious to join in. Most of the others knew each other by name and were showing their work or helping each other with problems. Sheila introduced herself and asked if I would be able to help her with a confusing part of the thumb on a mitten she was making.

With just a glance I could see that she had made some mistakes that weren't going to be easy to explain or correct. I've never felt that there's only one way to knit, or that there's only one way to deal with mistakes—whether in knitting or in life—so I decided to give her the choice about how to deal with them. I asked her if she wanted to rip out and reknit the mitten so it would be perfect, or if she wanted to just make it work somehow. I wasn't sure what her response would be, but Sheila liked being given a choice rather than being told what to do. In this instant, our friendship began.

Since then Sheila has become a very solid friend. She gives me her honest opinion if she thinks that a handle I've chosen for a purse design looks ugly. We both have grandchildren, but we have fun breaking knitting stereotypes about "grandmas in rocking chairs." You'll often find us on the bike trails along the American River, stopping for a picnic lunch and some knitting time, or cruising the yarn shops in her Jeep or my classic Mustang convertible. I need that kind of knitting friend!

# Helping Hand Mittens

I've designed a basic mitten using an "afterthought thumb" similar to the one Sheila was struggling with when we met. The thumb opening is created by knitting the thumb stitches with a long piece of scrap yarn, slipping those stitches back to the left needle and continuing to knit the rest of the hand as if nothing happened. Then at the very end, the scrap yarn is removed, leaving a hole and live stitches around it to pick up and knit the thumb. Have fun with it—and make a friend with it like I did.

---

SKILL LEVEL

Intermediate

SIZES

Fits Womens medium to large and Mens small to medium

FINISHED MEASUREMENTS

- Circumference (around hand): approximately 7½ inches
- Length: approximately 8 inches from fingertip to wrist

MATERIALS

- Naturally Vero [100% wool; 87 yd/80m per 50g skein], one skein 9 [A]
- Naturally Mist [80% super fine kid mohair / 20% nylon; 181 yd/166m per 25g skein], one skein 0608 [B]
- One yard of smooth cotton waste yarn, any color that contrasts with A (for stitch holder)
- One set of four or five US #7 (4.5mm) double-pointed needles
- Tapestry needle

GAUGE

18 sts and 24 rnds = 4 inches in Stockinette st with A

NOTES

Mittens are knit in the round beginning at the cuff. Stitches are left available for a thumb, which is knit last. Two identical mittens means there is neither a left mitten nor a right mitten.

DIRECTIONS

**Cuff**

Using B doubled, cast on 32 sts. Divide over 3 double-pointed needles and join, making sure not to twist. Place marker for beginning of round. Work knit 1 tbl, purl 1 ribbing every round for 3".

**Hand**

Change to A. Knit 16 rounds even.

## Thumb Opening

With strand of cotton waste yarn, knit first 6 sts of round.
Cut waste yarn and slip same 6 sts back to left-hand needle.
Continue to knit every round with A for 4".

## Fingertip Decreases

**Round 1:** *Knit 4, k2tog; repeat from * around.
**Round 2:** *Knit 3, k2tog; repeat from * around.
**Round 3:** *Knit 2, k2tog; repeat from * around.
**Round 4:** *Knit 1, k2tog; repeat from * around.
**Round 5:** *K2tog around.
Cut yarn, leaving a 12" tail. Using tapestry needle, thread
through remaining sts. Pull tight and fasten off yarn.

## Thumb

Remove waste yarn from thumb opening, leaving live stitches
above and below a hole. Put these sts on needles. Join yarn,
knit across 6 sts below hole, pick up 2 sts on side of hole,
knit across 5 sts across top of hole, pick up 2 sts on side of
hole—15 sts. Knit around, decreasing evenly to to 12 sts.
Knit every round for 12 rounds. Next round: K2tog around
next. Cut yarn, leaving a 12" tail. Using tapestry needle,
thread tail through remaining sts. Pull tight and fasten off
yarn. Weave in ends.

Make second mitten identical to first.

# NOTHING HAPPENS
## *by* ACCIDENT

After I had sold my yarn company, which required my involvement in every detail of the business, my new knitwear design venture seemed simple. I enjoyed designing garments, but it quickly became just one sweater after another, with little challenge or variety. I missed the creativity of developing new products, creating marketing plans, and attending trade shows, yet I didn't want to start another business, which would only consume my time and energy in the same ways that my yarn company had. I prayed for peace, purpose, and a definitive direction for my career.

Over one weekend, before leaving for a trade show, two exciting opportunities arose at the same time, both seemingly out of the blue. I had spoken with some author-friends about how to pursue the possibility of writing a book. I'd essentially given up because I just didn't know how to make it happen or whom to talk to, but prayed for purpose anyway. Minutes before I left for the airport, I got a call from an editor named Joy. A talented friend had given her my name and recommended that she talk to me. I gathered up my ideas and prepared to meet with Joy at the trade show. After more than fifteen years of selling yarn and teaching knitting workshops, I felt that I had at least one book in me, maybe more. Finding the right person to talk to and making it happen were not in my control, but Joy has held my hand and nudged me through the process of writing this book, always in the most positive and encouraging way.

While I was at the same trade show, a friend named Frederikka offered me a creative position within her yarn import company. I'd met her many years before at a small yarn show in Seattle. Like many small business owners, Frederikka had many more items on her to-do list than she had hours in the day to do them. She needed a right-hand woman, so to speak, to

discuss ideas, take charge of advertising, double-check that all her yarns were being marketed, find a way to launch her line of patterns, and provide support at trade shows. Her warehouse is about three hours from my home. Most of the work I do for her can be done via email or over the phone, with just an occasional drive to see her in person. I love the variety of tasks that I get to do, and Frederikka's friendship is a terrific fringe benefit.

Just as the other stories I share in this book are about real people and the way that my experiences with them are the pieces in the jigsaw puzzle of my life—pieces I don't even know I'm missing until I find them—my stories about Joy and Frederikka are just two small fragments of my life. I don't know how all the pieces fit together, and I'm too small to see the whole picture at once. Occasionally, as I did on that day, I get a glimpse of something bigger, and see how the pieces might fit. Someday it will be awesome to see the whole puzzle assembled.

## Multidirectional Socks

To extend the metaphor of life's puzzle, the pieces don't always fit together the way we think they will—or should. But when the pieces "snap" into place, it becomes obvious that it's the way it was meant to be. For this project I've designed a rather basic sock, but the method of construction is a bit unexpected. I started by knitting the leg portion horizontally, around the leg, instead of using the standard method. Simple puzzle pieces that still fit together to make a great, albeit untraditional, sock.

Intermediate

Baby (Adult)

- Circumference (leg): about 4 (8) inches
- Height (leg): about 2 (7) inches

- Aurora Yarns Steinbach Wolle Strapaz Norweger Ringel [80% wool, 20% polyamide; 164 yd/150m per 50g skein]
  - one skein color # 009 for baby
  - two skeins color #011 for adult
- Three yards sport weight cotton waste yarn
- Crochet hook size D-3 (3.25mm)
- One set of four US #1 (2.25mm) double-pointed needles
- Tapestry needle

28 sts and 44 rows = 4 inches in Stockinette st

Leg is knit from side to side, beginning with a temporary cast-on. The last row is then joined to the cast-on using either kitchener stitch or 3-needle bind-off. The foot sts are picked up and knit downward in the round from the leg section.

**Sideways Ribbing**

**Row 1 (RS):** Knit.

**Row 2:** Purl.

**Row 3:** Knit.

**Row 4:** Knit.

## Leg

With waste yarn and crochet hook, crochet a chain at least 18 (52) sts long. Using sock yarn and knitting needle, pick up and knit 16 (50) sts from back loop of chain. Purl one row. Work in Sideways Ribbing for 4 (7½)", do not bind off. Use either kitchener stitch or 3-needle bind-off to join last row to first row.

## Heel

Pick up and knit 36 (60) sts around edge of leg. Place 18 (30) sts on 2 needles for instep. Place remaining 18 (30) sts on one needle to work heel.

**Row 1:** *Slip1, k1; repeat from *.

**Row 2:** Slip 1, purl across row.

Repeat Rows 1 and 2 until heel flap measures 1½ (2¼)", ending with Row 2.

### Turn heel

**Row 1:** K10 (17), ssk, k1, turn.

**Row 2:** Slip 1, p5, p2tog, p1, turn.

**Row 3:** Slip 1, k6, ssk, k1, turn.

**Row 4:** Slip 1, p7, p2tog, p1, turn.

Continue in this way, working 1 more st between decs until all 18 (30) sts have been worked, ending with a WS row— 10 (18) sts.

## Instep

With 1st needle (#1) knit across heel sts, pick up and knit 9 (15) sts along edge of heel. With 2nd needle (#2) knit across next 18 (30) sts. With 3rd needle (#3) pick up and knit 9 (15)

## Gusset

**Round 1:** Needle #1—Knit to last 3 sts, k2tog, k1; Needle #2—work in pattern; Needle #3—k1, ssk, knit to end.

**Round 2:** Knit.

Repeat these two rounds until there are 9 (15) sts on Needles #1 and #3. Work even until sock measures 1 (1½)" shorter than foot length.

## Toe

**Round 1:** Needle #1—Knit to last 3 sts, k2tog, k1; Needle #2—Knit 1, ssk, knit to last 3 sts, k2tog, k1; Needle #3—Knit 1, ssk, knit to end.

**Round 2:** Knit.

Repeat these two rounds until 16 (20) sts remain.

Graft toe sts using kitchener st. Weave in ends.

# ABOVE and BEYOND

Sometimes yarn stores and knitting guilds coordinate the timing of their events so they can share an out-of-town teacher's travel expenses. On one of my trips to southern California, I flew out to teach for two groups: the Valley Needlers, a large knitting guild, and a nearby yarn shop. I didn't know anyone from either the guild or the store, not even the name of the person who would be picking me up at the airport.

Unfortunately this trip didn't start off well. The problems began where they usually do—at the airport. Who would think that a short flight from northern to southern California could become so miserably delayed? (This is exactly why I should pack food and makeup even if my trip is supposed to be the Gilligan's Island "three-hour tour.")

Eventually I did make it to my southern destination, where Donna, one of the guild members, was anxiously awaiting my arrival. She and her husband had waited patiently in spite of the long delay, then generously took me to dinner and drove me to my hotel. The next day I taught my all-day purse-making class, during which my two dozen fun, creative students told me about their guild activities. Much of the time in my classes is spent creating and playing, so we're able get to know each other and share stories. I was impressed with how charitable this group is with its knitting. Like many guilds, they use their knitting needles to support soldiers, the homeless, veterans, children, women's shelters, and countless other groups.

Another guild member, Ann, volunteered to take me to my next destination. As we talked during the drive to the yarn shop, we realized that we had our Christian faith in common, and agreed that the best thing about knitting is how it connects us to other people. Ann told me that she shares her gift of knitting by making hats for charities that support premature babies, homeless shelters, and special needs kids, as well as by teaching people how to knit. She even started her own after-school program to teach children how to knit. Ann described child after child who gained confidence and pride through the skills they learned, the projects they created, and the time they spent together.

# Charity Hat

To honor and celebrate the enthusiastic charitable missions of these two women and their knitting guild, I designed a feminine beanie that could be made for a local women's shelter or a chemo center. The yarn is very soft and comforting, and just enough texture to hide a bare scalp through the eyelet lace pattern.

For more information on how to connect with a knitting guild in your area, or for getting in touch with charities that supply knitted items to those suffering from life-threatening illnesses or who need special help, or charities that help abused women and children, refer to the Resources section on page 140.

## SKILL LEVEL
Intermediate

## SIZE
One size fits most (teens through adults)

## FINISHED MEASUREMENTS
Circumference: 18½ inches

## MATERIALS
- Lion Brand Cotton Ease [50% cotton, 50% acrylic; 207 yd/188m per 100g skein], one skein color #110 Lake
- One 16-inch US #7 (4.5mm) circular needle
- One 16-inch US #5 (3.75mm) circular needle
- One set of 4 or 5US #7 (4.5mm) double-pointed needles
- Stitch marker
- Tapestry needle

## GAUGE
17 sts and 28 rnds = 4 inches in Curving Lace patt

## STITCH PATTERN

KEY
- □ k on RS, p on WS
- ⊙ yo
- ☑ k2tog
- ◩ ssk

### Curving Lace Pattern (multiple of 5 sts)
**Round 1:** Knit.
**Round 2:** *K2tog, yo, k3; repeat from *.
**Round 3:** Knit.
**Round 4:** *Yo, ssk, k3; repeat from *.

## DIRECTIONS

Using smaller circular needle, cast on 85 sts. Join, being careful not to twist. Place marker to indicate beginning of round.

*Ribbing:* *Purl 2, k3; repeat from * around. Work 4 rounds of ribbing. Change to larger circular needle and work in Curving Lace patt for 5", ending after Round 4.

Shape the crown (changing to double-pointed needles when needed):

**Round 1:** Knit.

**Round 2:** *K2tog, yo, k2tog, k1; repeat from *.

**Round 3:** Knit.

**Round 4:** *Yo, ssk, k2; repeat from *.

**Round 5:** Knit.

**Round 6:** *K2tog, yo, k2tog; repeat from *.

**Round 7:** Knit.

**Round 8:** *Yo, ssk, k1, repeat from *.

**Round 9:** Knit.

**Round 10:** Slip last st of previous round back to left needle, *K3tog, yo; repeat from *.

**Round 11:** Knit.

**Round 12:** *Yo, ssk; repeat from *.

**Round 13:** Knit.

**Round 14:** *K2tog; repeat from *.

**Round 15:** Knit.

**Round 16:** *K2tog; repeat from *, end k1.

Cut yarn, leaving a 10" tail. Using tapestry needle, thread tail through remaining sts twice. Pull tight and fasten off yarn. Weave in ends.

# *a* BURDEN
# BORNE WELL

The observation that we're unable to control everything is supposed to give comfort and teach acceptance. Though I thought I knew what that meant, while I was teaching one weekend I truly controlled nothing and felt like everything was going wrong.

After suffering from migraines for years, I finally found a medication that would control them. Unfortunately for me—and for my students that day—that medication also short-circuited the connection between my brain and my mouth. My classes went terribly. I said things out of order and confused people. It was discouraging and frustrating, not to mention embarrassing. Of course none of my students understood why I was acting that way, and I didn't feel that I could explain what the problem was.

One of my students, a woman named Eileen, was unusually compassionate. She may not have realized it, but she raised my spirits just by finding the good in my class, and by sharing her ideas. During lunch, I confessed to her my frustration with the difficulties I was having with communicating clearly. Eileen was honest but sweet, at first saying that she had wondered why my instructions were so hard to follow, then making suggestions that would help the class run more smoothly. Her respect for my privacy and her refusal to judge me were heartening.

Eileen then confided that she was going through her own physical challenges. An illness had sapped her energy as well as her ability to think clearly, which made her feel as if she had lost her creativity. Working on her art would have given her some consolation, but the hurdle of getting started seemed too difficult to surmount while she was dealing with the assault on her body from her illness and its treatment. In spite of my deficiencies, my class ignited Eileen's creative spark. She said it had been a long time since she felt that spirit, and that it had triggered tremendous enthusiasm once again.

We each offered something the other needed, along with a desire to share it: Eileen needed to find a way into fun, and maybe a bit of healing, by reconnecting to her creativity, while I needed to regain my confidence to teach while dealing with the side effects of medication. I still feel comforted when I think back on that day. In hindsight, I wish I hadn't tried so hard to control something I couldn't, and to hide something that couldn't be hidden. Doing so left my students feeling confused or disappointed. If I had just admitted that I was having health problems, I would have been calmer and my class more patient with me. Clearly my pride was my downfall.

# Silver Linings Tote

Each time I teach my "Silver Linings" purse class, I end up creating a sample during the class to demonstrate the different steps. That way I'm giving my students a "hands-on" example along with my verbal instructions and written handouts. It also means that I now have a huge variety of purses! Every one begins as a simple rectangle of knitting, and this one is the same: A little tuck or fold to form the base, a zipper, and some pretty trim and handles and it becomes an original work of art. The most important detail is the lining; my fused lining technique stabilizes the knitted fabric, making it as practical as it is pretty.

---

SKILL LEVEL
Easy

SIZE
One size

FINISHED MEASUREMENTS
- Height: 13 inches
- Width: 16 inches

MATERIALS
- SouthWest Trading Company Yin [60% Wool/20% Silk/20% Bamboo; 165 yd/150m per 50g skein], one skein color #822 [A]
- SouthWest Trading Company Inspiration [50% Alpaca/50% Soy Silk; 126 yd/115m per 50g skein], one skein Be Real #396 [B]
- SouthWest Trading Company Vegas [67% Wool, 29% Soy Silk, 4% Lurex; 110 yd/100m per 50g skein], one skein Cirque #418 [C]
- SouthWest Trading Company Pure [100% Soy Silk; 165 yd/150m per 50g skein], one skein China Blue #077 [D]
- SouthWest Trading Company Bamboo [100% Bamboo; 275 yd/250m per 100g skein], one skein each
  - color #521-SAH [E]
  - Ocean Stripe 154 [H]
- SouthWest Trading Company Love [70% Bamboo, 30% Silk; 99 yd/90m per 50g skein], one skein Jack and Sally #248 [F]
- SouthWest Trading Company Yang [60% Wool/20% Silk/20% Bamboo with metallic sequins; 60 yd/55m per 50g skein], one skein color #836 [G]
- SouthWest Trading Company Rock [40% Soysilk, 30% Fine Wool, 30% Hemp; 110 yd/100m per 50g skein], one skein Trent #760 [I]

- US #5 (3.75mm) knitting needles
- Crochet hook size F-5 (3.75mm)
- Somerset Designs 24" Suede Handles, color Denim
- Somerset Designs Large Tote Bag Bottom, color Denim
- One skein embroidery floss to match suede
- One 1½" button
- ½ yards cotton fabric
- Two yards x 17"-wide HeatnBond Ultra Hold Iron-on Adhesive

- Iron
- Pins
- Tapestry needle

GAUGE

20 sts and 28 rows = 4 inches in Stockinette st

Bag is knit in one piece from side to side. The lining fabric is then fused on to the knitting, seamed, and inserted into a suede tote bottom.

## PATTERN AND COLOR SEQUENCE

Work rows and colors as indicated in Stockinette st (knit every RS row, purl every WS row).

6 rows A

4 rows B

10 rows C

4 rows D

10 rows E

14 rows F

6 rows  G

4 rows H

6 rows I

## DIRECTIONS

With A, cast on 65 sts. Work in stockinette following pattern as indicated. Work even, repeating pattern and color sequence until piece measures 33". Bind off. Steam block completely flat from the wrong side.

### Lining

Cut piece of HeatnBond 35" long and same width as knitting (approx 13"). Fuse to wrong side of fabric, following manufacturer's instructions. Allow to cool, then peel off paper backing. Place adhesive side of fabric down onto wrong side of knitting. Fuse in place, being careful not to heat the 2" of length that extends beyond the knit fabric.

Sew cast-on edge to bound-off edge. Holding iron inside the tube, fuse the 2" overlap.  Pin tube inside suede tote bottom, resting it even with the seam on the tote bottom. Sew in place using embroidery floss, and backstitch through the pre-punched holes.

### Upper Edge

With D, cast on 18 sts. Work in Stockinette st for 33". Bind off. Sew cast-on edge to bound-off edge. Steam block completely flat from the wrong side. Cut a piece HeatnBond to  3½" wide by 33" long, piecing the iron-on adhesive if necessary. Fuse to wrong side of knit strip, being careful to maintain precise length of strip. Fold strip in half lengthwise and pin in place around upper edge of tote. Fuse in place.

### Handles

Pin handles in place about 5" apart, centered on each side of tote. Sew in place using embroidery floss and backstitch through the pre-punched holes.

### Closure

Crochet a chain about 6" long. Attach to outside of bag, centered at the top edge between handles. Sew button to outside edge on front of bag, centered between handles.

# CUSHIONING *the* BLOW

I n 2006, three days before I was scheduled to teach at a big consumer knitting show, my father-in-law collapsed and died instantly of an aneurysm. Nothing could have shocked my family and me more.

As stunned as I was, I knew that I needed to make a decision: to teach at the show, or to bow out gracefully. I thought about what my father-in-law, who had worked his entire life as an educator, would have wanted. The day before my first class was to begin, I gathered my supplies and called the organizers of the show to let them know that I would be there to teach my classes. I excused myself from the social events of the weekend—the dinners and fashion shows—but I went prepared to teach.

Anyone who has experienced grief knows that it can hit you at any time, unexpectedly, especially when you think you're handling it just fine, so I told my students about what had happened. They were very understanding, and my classes went well.

In one class, a woman had brought in some beautiful, expensive beaded trim from India whose quality and style was exceptional. She wound off several yards of it and handed it to me. She knew about the stress I was under, trying to teach while still processing the reality of the situation, and that beads wouldn't change my grief. But she also knew that a small, tangible gift would reach my heart and make me feel cared-for. Though I had been holding up well, her unexpected generosity brought more tears—tears of appreciation instead of sadness.

# Comfort Pillow

Although the class I was teaching that day was about how to make purses, I've used the beaded fringe gift to accent a pillow. I like the idea of having a peaceful lace pillow as a memorial of the comfort and support that came during a time of shock and pain, and I also wanted to highlight the beauty of the beads and allow them to shine. A pillow, especially one knitted with silk, is inviting and comforting, and can be enjoyed every day of the year as it lends beauty to a room. The lace pattern is pretty but simple to execute, with only two rows to repeat. I sewed my own lining to match the color of the yarn, but you could also purchase a small, plain pillow and knit the lace to cover it.

---

SKILL LEVEL
Advanced

SIZE
One size

FINISHED MEASUREMENTS
12-inch square

MATERIALS
- Jade Sapphire Maju [100% silk; 85 yd/78m per 50g skein], three skeins Bing Bing Red 56
- Beaded trim on satin ribbon, 1½ yards
- US #8 (5mm) knitting needles
- Fiberfill stuffing
- ½ yard fabric
- Thread, sewing machine
- Tapestry needle

GAUGE

16 sts and 20 rows = 4 inches in Stockinette st

STITCH PATTERN

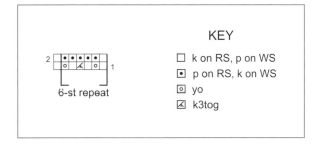

**KEY**

☐  k on RS, p on WS
☑  p on RS, k on WS
⊙  yo
☒  k3tog

6-st repeat

**Easy Lace (multiple of 6 + 1)**

**Row 1:** *Knit 1, yo, k1, k3tog, k1, yo; repeat from * until 1 st
remains, k1.

**Row 2:** *Purl 1, k5; repeat from * until 1 st remains, p1.

DIRECTIONS

**Front**

Cast on 43 sts. Work in Easy Lace Pattern until front
measures 12". Bind off.

**Back**

Cast on 48 sts. Work in stockinette until back measures 12".
Bind off. Weave in ends.

Cut 2 pieces of fabric each 13" square. Sew around edges
using a ½" seam allowance and leaving a 3" opening along
one side. Turn right side out. Fill with fiberfill and sew
opening closed.

Sew ribbon edge of beaded trim to edge of the fabric pillow.
Pin the front and back pieces to the fabric pillow around the
edges, leaving the beads loose. Sew all edges together.

# PASSING *it* ON

I find it ironic—and frustrating, of course—that sometimes when I think I have something very important to say I can't get anyone to listen, while other times, when I barely remember saying anything at all, my comments were apparently so significant that they inspired someone to make a major life change. When this happens, I know it isn't really the power of my words that changes people, but their own faith, and the confidence it can awaken.

I met Kimberly because she noticed that I was knitting in our Bible study class. She asked me if knitting was something she would be able to learn. I told her what I tell everyone who asks me that question: "Of course you can do it!" Did she ever—she actually taught herself to knit. Her first project was a hooded sweatshirt for her baby. And she did it all on her own, without classes or a teacher; she just went to a store, picked up a pattern booklet, yarn, and needles, and there she was: a knitter.

After conquering that first sweater, Kimberly was captivated. She knit dozens of others, then began knitting samples and designing patterns for yarn manufacturers. She soared to the "Experienced Knitter" level in just three short years.

How amazing it is to me that I can say "you can do it" to a hundred people, and though most of them will ignore me one will actually go out and do it. Kimberly was one of those people; my words, telling her that it was possible, were the nudge she needed to claim one of her gifts.

# Feminine Stretch Tank

In keeping with Kim's personality, style, and petite figure, I've designed a little tank top made with a stretchy elastic-blend yarn. The pattern requires some side-shaping, but the snug fit has a lot to do with the springy yarn, which hugs the body. The ribbon that laces up the front can be tightened (or loosened) according to how modest (or sexy) the wearer feels when she puts it on.

SKILL LEVEL
Intermediate

SIZES
Extra Small (Small, Medium, Large, Extra Large)

FINISHED MEASUREMENTS
- Bust: 32 (36, 40, 44, 48) inches
- Length: 20½ (21½, 22½, 23½, 24½) inches

MATERIALS
- Cascade Yarns Fixation [98.3% cotton, 1.7% elastic; 100 yd/110m per 50g skein], five (six, seven, eight, nine) skeins color #6399

- US #5 (3.75mm) knitting needles
- One 16-inch and one 29-inch US #5 (3.75mm) circular needles
- Stitch markers
- Three yards ⅜"-wide organza ribbon
- Seven hundred 3.75mm square beads with large holes
- Ten large decorative beads (larger than 3.75mm)
- Thin needles to string beads
- Tapestry needle

GAUGE
24 sts and 40 rows = 4 inches in Stockinette st

## DIRECTIONS

### Back

Cast on 96 (108, 120, 132, 144) sts.

**Row 1(WS):** Purl 22 (25, 31, 31, 34) sts, place marker, knit 1, place marker, purl 50 (56, 56, 68, 74) sts, place marker, knit 1, place marker, purl 22 (25, 31, 31, 34) sts. Row 2 (RS): Knit 22 (25, 31, 31, 34) sts, purl marked st, knit 50 (56, 56, 68, 74) sts, purl marked st, knit 22 (25, 31, 31, 34) sts.

Repeat Rows 1 and 2 and AT THE SAME TIME, decrease 1 st at each edge every 10th RS row 6 times—84 (96, 108, 120, 132) sts. Work even for 2". Increase 1 st at each edge every 10th RS row 6 times. Work even until body measures 14 (14½, 15, 15½, 16)" from cast-on edge.

### Shape Armholes

Bind off 9 (9, 12, 12, 12) sts at beg of next 2 rows. Dec 1 st at each end every RS row 9 (9, 12, 12, 12) times. Work even on 60 (72, 72, 84, 96) sts until armhole measures 5½ (6, 6½, 7, 7½)". Knit 9 (15, 15, 18, 21) sts for shoulder, join second ball of yarn, bind off center 42 (42, 42, 48, 54) sts for back neck, knit 9 (15, 15, 18, 21) sts for shoulder. Work each side separately for 1". Bind off 3 (5, 5, 6, 7) sts at shoulder edge 3 times.

### Left Front

Cast on 48 (54, 60, 66, 72) sts.

**Row 1 (WS):** Purl 22 (25, 31, 31, 34) sts, place marker, knit 1, place marker, purl 25 (28, 28, 34, 37) sts.

**Row 2 (RS):** Knit 25 (28, 28, 34, 37) sts, purl 1, knit 22 (25, 31, 31, 34) sts. Repeat Rows 1 and 2 AND AT THE SAME TIME, dec 1 st at side edge every 10th RS row 6 times—42 (48, 54, 60, 66) sts. Work even for 2". Increase 1 st at side edge every 10th RS row 6 times. Work even until body measures 14 (14½, 15, 15½, 16)" from cast-on edge, ending after a WS row.

### Shape Armhole and Neck

Bind off 9 (9, 12, 12, 12) sts. Dec 1 st at armhole edge every RS row 9 (9, 12, 12, 12) times and 1 st at neck edge every 4th row 11 (11, 11, 12, 13) times, then every RS row 10 (10, 10, 12, 13) times. Work even on 9 (15, 15, 18, 21) sts until armhole measures 6½ (7, 7½, 8, 8½)", ending at shoulder edge. Bind off 3 (5, 5, 6, 7) sts at shoulder edge 3 times.

### Right Front

Cast on 48 (54, 60, 66, 72) sts.

**Row 1 (WS):** Purl 25 (28, 28, 34, 37) sts, place marker, knit 1, place marker, purl 22 (25, 31, 31, 34) sts.

**Row 2 (RS):** Knit 22 (25, 31, 31, 34) sts, purl 1, knit 25 (28, 28, 34, 37) sts. Repeat Rows 1 and 2 AND AT THE SAME TIME, dec 1 st at side edge every 10th RS row 6 times—42 (48, 54, 60, 66) sts. Work even for 2". Increase 1 st at side edge every 10th RS row 6 times. Work even until body measures 14 (14½, 15, 15½, 16)" from cast-on edge, ending after a RS row.

### Shape Armhole and Neck

Bind off 9 (9, 12, 12, 12) sts. Dec 1 st at armhole edge every RS row 9 (9, 12, 12, 12) times and 1 st at neck edge every 4th row 11 (11, 11, 12, 13) times, then every RS row 10 (10, 10, 12, 13) times . Work even on 9 (15, 15, 18, 21) sts until armhole measures 6½ (7, 7½, 8, 8½)", ending at shoulder edge. Bind off 3 (5, 5, 6, 7) sts at shoulder edge 3 times.

Sew shoulders.

### Front and Neck Edging

With longer (29-inch) circular needle, and beginning at center right front edge, pick up and knit approximately 84 (87, 90, 93, 96) sts from lower edge to first neck decrease, 42 (45, 48, 52, 54) sts to shoulder, 54 (54, 54, 60, 66) across back neck, 42 (45, 48, 52, 54) sts from shoulder to bottom of neck shaping and 84 (87, 90, 93, 96) sts to lower front edge. Knit 1 row. *Yo, k2tog; repeat from * across row. Knit 1 row. Bind off.

String small square seed beads onto yarn end. Push 1 bead up to needle, bind off next stitch; repeat across all sts.

## Armhole edgings

With shorter (16-inch) circular needle, pick up and knit approximately 84 (90, 96, 104, 108) sts around armhole. Knit 1 row. *Yo, k2tog; repeat from * across row. Knit 1 row. Bind off.

String small square seed beads onto yarn end. Push 1 bead up to needle, bind off next stitch; repeat across all sts.

Sew side seams.

Weave in all ends.

Lace ³/₈" ribbon through eyelets of center front beginning at hem. Thread ribbon up front as far as desired. Put beads on each end of ribbon and tie knot.

Put 5 large decorative beads on each end of ribbon and tie knot.

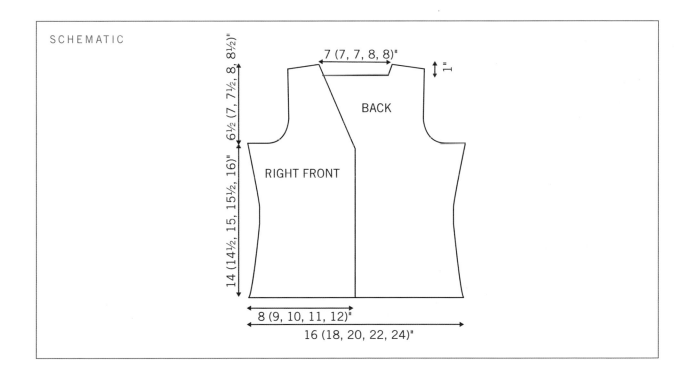

SCHEMATIC

# APPENDIX

## Skill Levels

**Beginner.** For first-time knitters. Uses basic knit and purl stitches. Minimal shaping is involved.

**Easy.** Uses basic stitches, repetitive stitch patterns, and simple color changes. Involves simple shaping and finishing.

**Intermediate.** Uses a variety of stitches, such as basic cables and lace, simple intarsia, double-pointed needles, and knitting-in-the-round needle techniques, with mid-level shaping and finishing.

**Experienced.** Involves intricate stitch patterns, techniques, and dimension, such as nonrepeating patterns, multicolored techniques, fine threads, detailed shaping, and refined finishing.

## Yarn Substitutions

The patterns in this book were each designed with a specific yarn in mind. If you substitute for a recommended yarn, you should choose one with the same weight and a similar fiber content. You should always take the time to make a gauge swatch before you begin a pattern, but it's especially important to do so if you are substituting for the suggested yarn. If necessary, change needle sizes to obtain the correct gauge.

| Yarn weight categories | 0 LACE | 1 SUPER FINE | 2 FINE | 3 LIGHT | 4 MEDIUM | 5 BULKY | 6 SUPER BULKY |
|---|---|---|---|---|---|---|---|
| **Types of yarn in category** | Fingering, 10-count crochet thread | Sock, fingering, baby | Sport, baby | DK, light worsted | Worsted, afghan, aran | Chunky, craft, rug | Bulky, roving |
| **Knit gauge range (in Stockinette stitch to 4 inches)** | 33–40 sts | 27–32 sts | 23–26 sts | 21–24 sts | 16–20 sts | 12–15 sts | 6–11 sts |
| **Recommended needle sizes (U.S./ metric sizes)** | 000–1/1.5–2.25mm | 1 to 3/ 2.25– 3.25mm | 3 to 5/ 3.25– 3.75mm | 5 to 7/ 3.75– 4.5mm | 7 to 9/ 4.5– 5.5mm | 9 to 11/ 5.5– 8mm | 11 and larger/ 8mm and larger |

Adapted from the Standard Yarn Weight System of the Craft Yarn Council of America.

## Basic Stitch Patterns

**Garter Stitch**

**Pattern Row:** Knit across.

   Repeat Patt Row.

**Stockinette Stitch**

**Row 1 (RS):** Knit across.

**Row 2:** Purl across.

   Repeat Rows 1 and 2.

## Knitting Abbreviations Key

**CC** = contrast color

**dec** = decrease

**est** = established

**inc** = increase

**k** = knit

**k2tog** = knit 2 together

**m** = meter

**MC** = main color

**oz** = ounce

**p** = purl

**p2tog** = purl 2 together

**psso** = pass slipped stitch over

**rnd** = round

**RS** = right side

**ssk** = slip the first and second stitches knitwise, one at a time, then insert the tip of left-hand needle into the fronts of these two stitches from the left, and knit them together from this position

**st** = stitch

**sts** = stitches

**WS** = wrong side

**yd** = yards

**yo** = yarn over

# Metric Conversion Charts

**Inches to Centimeters**

| Inches | CM | Inches | CM | Inches | CM | Inches | CM |
|--------|------|--------|-------|--------|--------|--------|--------|
| 1/16 | 0.16 | 13 | 33.02 | 40 | 101.60 | 67 | 170.18 |
| 1/8 | 0.32 | 14 | 35.56 | 41 | 104.14 | 68 | 171.72 |
| 3/16 | 0.48 | 15 | 38.10 | 42 | 106.68 | 69 | 175.25 |
| 1/4 | 0.64 | 16 | 40.64 | 43 | 109.22 | 70 | 177.80 |
| 5/16 | 0.79 | 17 | 43.18 | 44 | 111.76 | 71 | 180.34 |
| 3/8 | 0.95 | 18 | 45.72 | 45 | 114.30 | 72 | 182.88 |
| 7/16 | 1.11 | 19 | 48.26 | 46 | 116.84 | 73 | 185.42 |
| 1/2 | 1.27 | 20 | 50.80 | 47 | 119.38 | 74 | 187.96 |
| 9/16 | 1.43 | 21 | 53.34 | 48 | 121.92 | 75 | 190.50 |
| 5/8 | 1.59 | 22 | 55.88 | 49 | 124.46 | 76 | 193.04 |
| 11/16 | 1.75 | 23 | 58.42 | 50 | 127.00 | 77 | 195.58 |
| 3/4 | 1.91 | 24 | 60.96 | 51 | 129.54 | 78 | 198.12 |
| 13/16 | 2.06 | 25 | 63.50 | 52 | 132.08 | 79 | 200.66 |
| 7/8 | 2.22 | 26 | 66.04 | 53 | 134.62 | 80 | 203.20 |
| 15/16 | 2.38 | 27 | 60.58 | 54 | 137.16 | 81 | 205.74 |
| 1 | 2.54 | 28 | 71.12 | 55 | 139.70 | 82 | 208.28 |
| 2 | 5.08 | 29 | 73.66 | 56 | 142.24 | 83 | 210.82 |
| 3 | 7.65 | 30 | 76.20 | 57 | 144.78 | 84 | 213.26 |
| 4 | 10.16 | 31 | 78.74 | 58 | 147.32 | 85 | 215.90 |
| 5 | 12.70 | 32 | 81.28 | 59 | 149.86 | 86 | 218.44 |
| 6 | 15.24 | 33 | 83.82 | 60 | 152.40 | 87 | 220.98 |
| 7 | 17.78 | 34 | 86.36 | 61 | 154.94 | 88 | 223.52 |
| 8 | 20.32 | 35 | 88.90 | 62 | 157.48 | 89 | 226.05 |
| 9 | 22.66 | 36 | 91.44 | 63 | 160.02 | 90 | 228.60 |
| 10 | 25.40 | 37 | 93.98 | 64 | 162.56 | | |
| 11 | 27.94 | 38 | 96.52 | 65 | 165.10 | | |
| 12 | 30.48 | 39 | 99.06 | 66 | 167.64 | | |

## Centimeters to Inches

| Inches | CM | Inches | CM | Inches | CM | Inches | CM |
|---|---|---|---|---|---|---|---|
| 1 | $3/8$ | 40 | $15\,3/4$ | 79 | $31\,1/8$ | 118 | $46\,1/2$ |
| 2 | $3/4$ | 41 | $16\,1/8$ | 80 | $31\,1/2$ | 119 | $46\,7/8$ |
| 3 | $1\,1/8$ | 42 | $16\,1/2$ | 81 | $31\,7/8$ | 120 | $47\,1/4$ |
| 4 | $1\,5/8$ | 43 | $16\,7/8$ | 82 | $32\,1/4$ | 121 | $47\,5/8$ |
| 5 | $2$ | 44 | $17\,1/4$ | 83 | $32\,5/8$ | 122 | $48$ |
| 6 | $2\,3/8$ | 45 | $17\,3/4$ | 84 | $33$ | 123 | $48\,3/8$ |
| 7 | $2\,1/4$ | 46 | $18\,1/8$ | 85 | $33\,1/2$ | 124 | $48\,7/8$ |
| 8 | $3\,1/8$ | 47 | $18\,1/2$ | 86 | $33\,7/8$ | 125 | $49\,1/4$ |
| 9 | $3\,1/2$ | 48 | $18\,7/8$ | 87 | $34\,1/4$ | 126 | $49\,5/8$ |
| 10 | $4$ | 49 | $19\,1/4$ | 88 | $34\,5/8$ | 127 | $50$ |
| 11 | $4\,3/8$ | 50 | $19\,5/8$ | 89 | $35$ | 128 | $50\,3/8$ |
| 12 | $4\,3/4$ | 51 | $20$ | 90 | $35\,1/2$ | 129 | $50\,3/4$ |
| 13 | $5\,1/8$ | 52 | $20\,1/2$ | 91 | $35\,7/8$ | 130 | $51\,1/8$ |
| 14 | $5\,1/2$ | 53 | $20\,7/8$ | 92 | $36\,1/4$ | 131 | $51\,5/8$ |
| 15 | $5\,7/8$ | 54 | $21\,1/4$ | 93 | $36\,5/8$ | 132 | $52$ |
| 16 | $6\,1/4$ | 55 | $21\,5/8$ | 94 | $37$ | 133 | $52\,3/8$ |
| 17 | $6\,3/4$ | 56 | $22$ | 95 | $37\,3/8$ | 134 | $52\,3/4$ |
| 18 | $7\,1/8$ | 57 | $22\,1/2$ | 96 | $37\,3/4$ | 135 | $53\,1/8$ |
| 19 | $7\,1/2$ | 58 | $22\,7/8$ | 97 | $38\,1/4$ | 136 | $53\,1/2$ |
| 20 | $7\,7/8$ | 59 | $23\,1/4$ | 98 | $38\,5/8$ | 137 | $53\,7/8$ |
| 21 | $8\,1/4$ | 60 | $23\,5/8$ | 99 | $39$ | 138 | $54\,3/8$ |
| 22 | $8\,5/8$ | 61 | $24$ | 100 | $39\,3/8$ | 139 | $54\,3/4$ |
| 23 | $9$ | 62 | $24\,3/8$ | 101 | $39\,3/4$ | 140 | $55\,1/8$ |
| 24 | $9\,1/2$ | 63 | $24\,3/4$ | 102 | $40\,1/8$ | 141 | $55\,1/2$ |
| 25 | $9\,7/8$ | 64 | $25\,1/4$ | 103 | $40\,1/2$ | 142 | $55\,7/8$ |
| 26 | $10\,1/4$ | 65 | $25\,5/8$ | 104 | $41$ | 143 | $56\,1/2$ |
| 27 | $10\,5/8$ | 66 | $26$ | 105 | $41\,3/8$ | 144 | $56\,3/4$ |
| 28 | $11$ | 67 | $26\,3/8$ | 106 | $41\,3/4$ | 145 | $57$ |
| 29 | $11\,3/8$ | 68 | $26\,3/4$ | 107 | $42\,1/8$ | 146 | $57\,1/2$ |
| 30 | $11\,7/8$ | 69 | $27\,1/8$ | 108 | $42\,1/2$ | 147 | $57\,7/8$ |
| 31 | $12\,1/4$ | 70 | $27\,1/2$ | 109 | $42\,7/8$ | 148 | $58\,1/4$ |
| 32 | $12\,5/8$ | 71 | $28$ | 110 | $43\,1/4$ | 149 | $58\,5/8$ |
| 33 | $13$ | 72 | $28\,3/8$ | 111 | $43\,3/4$ | 150 | $59$ |
| 34 | $13\,3/8$ | 73 | $28\,3/4$ | 112 | $44\,1/8$ | 151 | $59\,1/2$ |
| 35 | $13\,3/4$ | 74 | $29\,1/8$ | 113 | $44\,1/2$ | 152 | $59\,7/8$ |
| 36 | $14\,1/8$ | 75 | $29\,1/2$ | 114 | $44\,7/8$ | 153 | $60\,1/4$ |
| 37 | $14\,5/8$ | 76 | $29\,7/8$ | 115 | $45\,1/4$ | | |
| 38 | $15$ | 77 | $30\,1/4$ | 116 | $45\,5/8$ | | |
| 39 | $15\,3/8$ | 78 | $30\,3/4$ | 117 | $46$ | | |

# Knitting Needle Conversions

| Metric Sizes | U.S. Sizes | UK/Canadian Sizes |
|---|---|---|
| 2mm | 0 | 14 |
| 2.25mm | 1 | 13 |
| 2.75mm | 2 | 12 |
| 3.25mm | 3 | 10 |
| 3.5mm | 4 | - |
| 3.75mm | 5 | 9 |
| 4mm | 6 | 8 |
| 4.5mm | 7 | 7 |
| 5mm | 8 | 6 |
| 5.5mm | 9 | 5 |
| 6mm | 10 | 4 |
| 6.5mm | 10½ | 3 |
| 8mm | 11 | 0 |
| 9mm | 13 | 00 |
| 10mm | 15 | 000 |
| 12.75mm | 17 | - |
| 15mm | 19 | - |
| 19mm | 35 | - |
| 25mm | 50 | - |

# RESOURCES

## YARN

**Art Yarns**
39 Westmoreland Avenue
White Plains, NY 10606
914-428-0333
sales@artyarns.com
www.artyarns.com

**Aurora Yarns**
P. O. Box 3068
Moss Beach, CA 94038
650-728-2730
aurorayarns@pacbell.net
www.aurorayarns.net

**Brown Sheep Company, Inc.**
100662 County Road 16
Mitchell, NE 69357
800-826-9136
www.brownsheep.com

**Caron International**
P.O. Box 222
Washington, NC 27889
public_relations@caron.com
www.caron.com/contact

**Cascade Yarns**
www.cascadeyarn.com

**Heirloom**
Russi Sales, Inc.
605 Clark Road
Bellingham, WA 98225
rsi@nas.com
www.russisales.com

**Jade Sapphire**
866-857-3897
info@jadesapphire.com
www.jadesapphire.com

**Knit One, Crochet Too, Inc.**
91 Tandberg Trail, Unit 6
Windham, ME 04062
207-892-9625
info@knitonecrochettoo.com
www.knitonecrochettoo.com

**Lion Brand**
135 Kero Road
Carlstadt, NJ 07072
800-258-YARN
www.lionbrand.com

**Lorna's Laces**
4229 North Honore Street
Chicago, IL 60613
773-935-3803
yarn@lornaslaces.net
www.lornaslaces.net

**Naturally New Zealand Yarns**
Distributed in the US by Fiber Trends, Inc.
315 Colorado Park Place
East Wenatchee, WA 98802
509.884.8631
888.733.5991
email: bev@fibertrends.com
www.fibertrends.com

**Patons**
320 Livingstone Avenue South
Listowel, ON N4W 3H3
Canada
1-888-368-8401
inquire@spinriteyarns.com
www.patonsyarns.com

**S.W.T.C. Inc.**
www.soysilk.com

**Tanglewood Fiber Creations**
www.tanglewoodfibercreations.com

**Universal Yarns**
284 Ann Street
Concord, NC 28025
704-789-Yarn (9276)
877-UniYarn (864-9276)
sales@universalyarn.com
www.universalyarn.com

## KNITTING NOTIONS

**JHB International Buttons**
1955 South Quince Street
Denver, CO 80231
800-525-9007
www.buttons.com

**Zipperstop**
**Feibusch Corp.**
27 Allen Street
New York, NY 10002

Tel: 1-212/226-3964
888-947-7872
afeibusch@prodigy.net
www.zipperstop.com

## SUEDE PRODUCTS FOR KNITTERS

**Somerset Designs**
P.O. Box 425
Somerset, CA 95684
530-622-6898
somersetdesigns@yahoo.com
www.somersetdesigns.com

# INDEX

Note: **Bold** page numbers indicate projects.